It's in my Genes

Kathy Gillcrist

Pulse, LLC—Carolina Shores, NC
ISBN: 978-0-578-78812-8
Library of Congress Control Number: 2020921499
Title: *It's in my Genes*
Author: Kathy Gillcrist
Digital distribution | 2020
Paperback | 2020

Dedication

This book is dedicated to adoptees, adoptive parents, and all unselfish women who have made the difficult choice to surrender a child. I thank both of my mothers: one of birth and the other of heart. Each of you gave me the best of yourselves.

To my friends and family who have listened to more of this story than you ever wanted to hear: thank you for your patience and enthusiasm. I love you for listening.

To my cousin Susan Tupper Gillmor, my first biological connection and greatest cheerleader: not only were you a tireless detective, but a generous and meticulous editor. Without you, there would be no story. I am so grateful to have you as family and friend.

Introduction

I am a sixty-three year old drama queen who found her birth father on the FBI's Most Wanted List. After taking an Ancestry.com spit test, genealogical research concluded that my father is the famous murderer, William Bradford Bishop. The unsolved case of the gruesome Bishop Murders has fascinated true crime enthusiasts since 1976. Brad Bishop has been the subject of news reports, television programs and even a ballad. Although alleged sightings have popped up sporadically over the past forty years, he has remained elusive, keeping the mystery alive. My discovery adds yet another layer to his profile.

Brad's nefarious past is only part of my story. My birth mother's history is dramatic in its own right. A 23&Me test led me to discover her, as well as five shocked half siblings. None of them ever expected there was a sixth sibling, especially the daughter of a murderer. My birth mother kept that secret locked up tightly for over sixty years. Obviously, a penchant for intrigue exists on both sides of my biological family. *No wonder they produced a drama queen!*

In addition to an innate desire to entertain, my motivation for writing this book was to share observations about the formation of a person's identity. As an adopted child, I grew up noticing keen differences between myself and the other members of my adoptive family. They were quiet and unassuming; I was bold and attention-seeking. I was ambitious; they were pragmatic. As a parent and educator, I'm very familiar with the conflict between nature and nurture in identity development. I've always wondered just how much of one's identity develops through nurturing, and what traits are inherited through DNA. In this book, I've described my formative years and the character traits I developed. I've also analyzed the backgrounds of both sets of parents, and I concluded that the influences of both nature and nurture equally combined to create the unique person that I am. Searching for my biological family was not only an entertaining interlude in my life, but it also solidified my sense of identity.

I would love to claim full responsibility for digging up all the juicy information I learned about my birth parents, but I can't take credit for it. As luck would have it, the first genetic contact I made through my 23andMe test was with my third cousin Susan. She has proved to be not only a dear friend, but also an expert genealogist. In her own words, she clearly explains the methodology she used to draw up my biological trees. I'm sure her portion of the book will inspire those who wish to embark on their own genetic journey.

Everything I've written, to the best of my recollection, is true. Susan Tupper Gilmor is using her given name, but I have changed the names of my birth mother and half siblings in order to preserve their anonymity. They are gracious people and deserve privacy. Brad Bishop, of course, is responsible for his own notoriety, so I have no qualms about revealing his true name. As for my adoptive parents, their name is too distinctive to change, and they have nothing to hide. Most of the life experiences described in this memoir made me who I am. The rest was in my genes.

Part One
The Making of a Drama Queen

Even when I stopped chasing it, drama always found me.

I was a bossy little girl with a vivid imagination. Born with a type A personality, I was driven to succeed and determined to be exceptional. I remember informing my preschool playmates that their parents were stuck with them, but I was *chosen*. I was an adopted child with a fiercely competitive attitude.

Back in the 1950s, adoptive families were given a book called *The Chosen Baby*. The cover featured a dimpled, curly-haired infant floating across an azure sky. Obviously this cherub was heaven-sent. I came across a copy once at a church basement book sale, and I wondered how effective it had been in its quest to establish positive self esteem in adopted children. Decades had passed since I'd seen a copy of that book, but viewing it caused a sudden flash of nostalgia. One day my mom asked me if I remembered the first time she read it to me. In her memory, the event was an early bonding experience, and she hoped it had made me feel special. Sadly, I can't recall the incident, but it seemed very clear that my self esteem was always firmly in check...with or without the help of the floating cherub. I never doubted my destiny to become a star.

I was born on June 15, 1957, in Boston, Massachusetts. According to adoption records from The New England Home for Little Wanderers, I weighed 8 pounds, 9 3/4 ounces. *See. I was born a big shot.* Either my birth mother had been subjected to an extensive interview, or she was a natural chatterbox because she provided quite a bit of background information. When I was in my forties, I learned that a transcript of non-identifying information was available for my perusal. For a variety of reasons, I had never before felt a need to search for my birth parents. For one thing, I was afraid I might hurt my adoptive parents' feelings. With their blessing, however, curiosity quickly won over my hesitation. I whipped out my Visa card and ordered the file from the agency. I made the following discoveries: My given name was Darlene Marie. My birth mother was named Louise. I was her second daughter. She had been married briefly to the father of her first child, but not to mine. Louise reported that my father was named Donald, and he was separated from his first wife. She provided quite a few details about Donald, his Nordic heritage and his love of playing the drums. This was handy information, explaining my fair complexion and my daughter's talent for tap-dancing. I also learned that Donald had two sons from his first marriage, and I entertained thoughts of meeting some half brothers.

My birth mother claimed that her father would have preferred a son. Since she had no siblings, she felt that she was a disappointment to him. She said he was very strict, ordering her to leave home during the second pregnancy. She mentioned little about her mother, except that she was very petite. I interpreted this as an explanation for my second-born daughter's tiny bone structure. (Neither myself nor my husband had a petite gene in our bodies.) The document also indicated that she returned two years later with a third daughter. *What a busy girl.*

As was usually the case in 1957, I spent a few months with a foster family before I was adopted. My foster mother recorded that at 17 weeks, "this girl was tall and heavily built with weight reported at 19 pounds." *It was clear I was headed for the Pretty Plus department at Sears.* "Her round face had fat cheeks. Square hands had tapering fingers and her feet were thick at the instep. She had deep wrinkles at the joints and dimples, including one on her chin when she cried." To put it nicely, I guess I could have been described as a sturdy child; I sure didn't resemble the cover girl from *The Chosen Baby*. The foster mother later added that my "facial features were dainty and pretty." I'm glad she mentioned at least one redeeming quality.

According to my adoptive mother, when she first laid eyes on me I was a chubby, bald baby with big blue eyes and a huge grin. My gender was indicated by a giant green bow taped to the top of my head. *Apparently I already appreciated the importance of accessorizing.* Back in the old days, unwed mothers were not encouraged to raise their babies on their own. Adoption was a common practice among infertile couples who desired families. Agencies did their best to match orphans with parents who shared physical characteristics and common heritage. When I imagine my adoptive parents' visit to that orphanage, I envision a situation not unlike a modern day trip to a humane society shelter. Potential parents would stroll by the cribs and pick out the baby who spoke to them. My giant hair bow was screaming, "Pick me!"

On December 5, 1957, the $25.00 deposit fee was paid, and I was placed on trial with my adoptive parents, John (Jack) and Norma Sidebottom and a big brother named John. Since Norma and Jack had already adopted a child, they knew the drill. Except for a rash indicating a wool allergy, they thought I was a perfect fit. The trial adoption process moved smoothly. They named me Kathy Ann, and a new birth certificate was typed up. The old one was kept on file, however, and "con. to Sidebottom 12/61" was hand-written across the text. I assume the abbreviation stood for convert. I think the informality of the hand-written note across the top is kind of quaint. In any case, on December 19, 1958, Jack and Norma paid off the $50.00 adoption fee balance and I was legally theirs. We have since agreed that they got their money's worth.

I was never told otherwise, so I assume my brother adapted well to the family transition. He was a bit confused, however, about when I would start to look like a girl. Since it took a few years for my platinum blonde hair to grow in, my mother said my head resembled a hard boiled egg when I was sleeping. I think she meant it in a nice way. My brother's curiosity was satisfied when I finally acquired some eyebrows and a head full of straight, fine hair. I think Norma and Jack had been a little worried that I might be permanently bald. What else would have motivated my mother to cut some of my hair off and save it in an envelope? I came across the envelope decades later as I was cleaning my mother's kitchen. There it was, stuffed in the back of the junk drawer. I've kept it ever since. I'm not sure why I saved that envelope, but if anyone needs to cast a voodoo spell, I have some ancient hair of an infant to contribute.

My brother and I were the last of the Sidebottom kids to grow up in Stoughton, Massachusetts. Both my mom and my dad were raised in that town. Dad had been one of five children. There were sixteen years between my dad and his oldest sister, so we had cousins of all ages. Some of the cousins had children our age, so the lineage was often confusing. It seemed like children were always being added to the family tree, biologically or through adoption. My grandmother and a cousin had also raised several foster children. Needless to say, the Sidebottom family embraced a liberal attitude toward family. Everyone was accepted into the tribe. Most of us shared fair hair and complexions, but nobody was quite like me.

With a name like Sidebottom, people tend to know who you are. As one might suspect, there are many issues associated with such a distinctive surname. We were raised in the days before Bully Intervention Programs, and hearing "Sidetop, Bottom-sides, or Sideswipe" was a regular occurrence. Coping mechanisms at that time involved developing a good sense of humor or a strong left hook. I applied the first strategy; the second worked out pretty well for my brother. I really hated that surname. During my obnoxious pre-adolescent years, I would whine about ending up with the wrong people. I remember telling my parents, "I was supposed to be a Smith or a Jones or the princess of a small island nation." That last name was one dramatic characteristic that I didn't embrace.

To make matters worse, there were five Kathys in my elementary school class. Since my name was not a variation of Kathleen or Katherine, I was often forced to use both my first and last name or be called just plain Kathy. That choice was obvious. Just plain Kathy would never bring me the notoriety I so desperately sought. Mom thought I should have used Kathy Ann, but that implied a cuteness that my stocky frame and my bossy disposition just didn't support. I tried variations on the spelling, but it didn't help much, and it wasn't quite legal. I was repeatedly asked for my real name, or "what was Kathy short for?" It got tiring. In graduate school I toyed with the idea of legally changing it to Katherine. My mom, however, preferred Kathleen. It wasn't worth arguing over, so I stuck with Kathy Ann. But it still sounds wimpy to me, and I envy those who are blessed with distinguished names.

As I grew up, my already vivid imagination expanded exponentially. Our house was situated on a main road and we didn't have much of a neighborhood. There were a few boys around, but there weren't any other girls to play with. My brother and his friends seemed to be always busy doing uninteresting boy things, so I was left to amuse myself. That wasn't such a bad thing - I'd always found myself to be immensely entertaining. It also meant I had the starring role in all my fantasy productions.

Most of my fantasies involved my future as the next great star. For a while, I envisioned myself as the successor to Shirley Temple. Unfortunately, my parents were neither willing nor able to pay for tap-dancing lessons. But I was sure I could teach myself. My mother told me later, "We didn't really think you had any aptitude for dancing lessons, so we wanted to spare you the embarrassment." Remember the wide instep of my foot reported at birth? Plus, my dimples were in the wrong place. I also had no chance of ever getting banana curls like Shirley's. As a matter of fact, once I grew enough hair to cover my egg head, mom made several pitiful attempts at making my hair curl. Many a Toni home perm applied on Saturday night flattened by the end of Sunday school class. Sometimes, on the night before school pictures were scheduled, I'd sleep with hair tape stuck in my head in an effort to make the edges of my pixie cut curl in. That was the best we could do. The result looked kind of cute if you didn't notice the glue residue left on my cheeks. Or the crazy uneven bangs my mom created when she trimmed. Nevertheless, I was still convinced that my discovery and ensuing career was imminent, and all my faculties were focused on making that happen. Hoping to speed up the process, I regularly performed my own version of a tap dance solo on top of the picnic table in the backyard, waiting for a Hollywood agent to drive by. Once in a while my performance was regaled by a honk or a beep. *Obviously an adoring fan*, but it became apparent that destiny would need a while to kick in.

I've often wondered why my mother never discouraged my tabletop revues. Maybe she was just happy that I was outside. I'm sure she was pleased to see me get some exercise. It might be that I scheduled my performances to coincide with the airing of her favorite soap opera, *As The World Turns*. The hour from 1:00-2:00 pm was the sacred break time of many housewives during the 1960s. When their program was on, we children were required to entertain ourselves. The most probable reason, though, was that mom really did need a respite from Chatty Kathy's incessant conversation.

I was never an outdoorsy type of kid, but my parents had strong ideas about the value of fresh air. They went to great lengths to encourage my appreciation of nature. (And get me out of the house.) Although my mom denied it, I remember being told to go "talk with the trees," and I'm sure that on at least one occasion, the porch door didn't get locked by accident. Once my parents bought me a pogo stick, but they later worried I might shake my brains out. For a short time, I envisioned a future career as a tightrope walker until I pulled down the clothesline. Several years later, during my Peggy Fleming stage, my dad constructed a little ice-skating rink for me, and I traded my fake tap shoes for figure skates. I abandoned Shirley Temple for Peggy Fleming as my new idol. To my relief, Peggy had nice straight hair, so banana curls were no longer required. I had moved on to a greater challenge than tap-dancing - now I would become an Olympic figure skater. As soon as I mastered half of a figure eight, I would execute that and my stunning twirls (*or more likely just a twirl*) for all the oncoming traffic. Luckily, the ice melted before I generated too much embarrassment for my family. During the summer Olympics, I substituted gymnastics for figure skating. We had a metal swing set with uneven parallel bars. As one might imagine, I was as fine a gymnast and skater as I was a tap-dancer. Every now and then a passing car would still issue an appreciative beep, further enhancing my enthusiasm. *Or so I believed.* It was nice to hear from my adoring fans, but I wondered why that Hollywood agent still hadn't found me.

Not only did celebrity stars fascinate me, but also those of the celestial variety. During much of my childhood, America was engaged in the Space Race, and all forms of media featured references to abstract galaxies, extraterrestrials and the supernatural. In the evenings, our family often gathered around our black and white television (complete with aluminum foil wrapped antenna). *The Wonderful World of Disney* and The *Lawrence Welk Show* were very popular, but so was *The Twilight Zone, One Step Beyond, My Favorite Martian* and *Lost in Space.* When my bedtime rolled around, I would retreat to my upstairs bedroom overlooking the backyard hill. As my parents continued watching television downstairs, the sounds of their shows would drift up into my room. I was easily lulled asleep by the white noise of commercial programming. I'm not sure whether it happened when I was asleep or awake, but at some point I managed to concoct yet another theory that proved I was unique. I convinced myself that I was part of an alien experiment. According to my hypothesis, extraterrestrials had disguised themselves as humans and placed me in the orphanage. It was only a matter of time before the Mother Ship would park itself on my backyard hill and collect me for further study. This process would involve a brief suspension of time on Earth, heralded by the muting of the television. They would squeeze themselves through my bedroom window, whisk me from my bed and take me to their leader. Looking back on that experience, I'm thankful for an early bedtime and the consistency of my parents' television habit. I always fell asleep before the television was turned off. As an adult, it took a long time for me to learn to sleep without a television droning in the background. I wonder if my poor sleeping habits were a result of residual alien anxiety.

Although my parents were aware of my clever inventiveness, they didn't comprehend the full power of my creative genes. On more than one occasion I overheard myself referred to as "high strung". I wasn't sure what that meant, but I could tell by my mother's tone of voice that it was a quality she hoped I'd overcome. So, I never told anyone about my alien fantasy. I was sure they would have laughed and said I was too smart for such a silly idea. Among the documents supplied by the adoption agency were the results of an early IQ screening. Mine stated that "the child is bright and capable of higher education," and Norma and Jack were dedicated to fulfilling my cognitive needs. My parents always watched their pennies closely, but they did their very best to provide whatever cerebral enrichment they could. They had high expectations and I was eager to please.

My mom was a reader, and we regularly visited the library. I became an early reader, too, so I was provided with much praise and encouragement in that department. I remember when my beloved grandfather told me that reading would take me very far. I was ready to go. As I mentioned before, we didn't live in a neighborhood full of playmates, so I spent most of my time at home with my family. Public kindergarten was not funded by the school system at that time, but I was indulged in a part time nursery school program. Twice a week I visited Mrs. Holmes' home nursery school. I remember loving it there: she had a full-sized stuffed brown bear who growled when you pulled a string and a house full of kids. Every Tuesday and Thursday I would dress up in a puffy little dress and jump headfirst into preschool.

Not only was I given the opportunity to fulfill my intellectual development at Mrs. Holmes' Nursery School, but my artistic and dramatic genes were also given free reign. My most vivid memory is of the day I spilled something all over my dress. I'm sure I had set my mind to excel at finger painting and, in my enthusiasm, I got paint all over me. My dress had to be removed and laundered, and I spent the morning wearing nothing but a big shirt over my petticoat. It probably belonged to Mr Holmes...if there was one. Perhaps another child might be embarrassed, but not Kathy Ann. In my mind, my petticoat became a tutu, and I morphed into a ballerina for the day. The inspiration came from a set of ballet paper dolls I had at home. Their feet were permanently arranged in first position. Most likely I walked like that for the rest of the day. I can only guess my mom's reaction when she came to pick me up. The recap of my antics probably made her cringe, but it wouldn't be the last time. I'm sure I was very proud of my performance, even if I was lacking applause.

Enrollment in public school made my competitiveness swell. I attended the first two grades in a very small neighborhood school, so it wasn't hard to make myself stand out. It was literally a two room schoolhouse with the first grade class located directly across from the second grade. We all walked to school in the morning, walked home again for lunch, and returned for the afternoon. In the winter, we brought lunches from home and ate at our desks. I loved every minute of every day, *except maybe gym class,* and I was determined to be the smartest girl in the first grade. Since there were less than 15 competitors for the title, it wasn't a difficult goal. It didn't occur to me to challenge the boys until several years later. The year was 1963 after all.

Poor Mrs. Murphy, my first official school teacher; I'm sure I drove her nuts. A *Peanuts* fan would swear I was the model for Lucy. In contrast, my older brother John had not been a fan of the first-grade teacher. Years before school even started he had convinced me that my life would be miserable from the moment I entered her classroom until the end of the day. I'm sure that just added fuel to my fire. Instead, I adored school, Mrs. Murphy, and every teacher I ever had. (There is one exception, but we'll get to him later.) I loved the feel of the giant pencils, the squeak of the chalk on the board and the taste of white paste. *I ate a lot of white paste over the years, and I swear I can still smell it in elementary school classrooms.* At a parent/teacher conference, my mother was told that I needed to be given extra work in order to stay busy. Mom was proud of her smart little girl; she didn't realize that was code for "your child is obnoxious." Unlike most kids and Sidebottoms, my brain worked quickly, and my attention span was short.

For second grade, we migrated across the hall to the other room. We felt very grown up. For one thing, second graders were allowed to walk downstairs to the restroom by themselves. It was simply called the basement. It contained a noisy furnace, lots of water pipes, a boy's room and a girl's room. We were entrusted with the skeleton key that unlocked the door. ADHD had not been invented then, so what I suffered from was called ants in my pants. The best remedy for all involved was a change of scenery, so I visited the basement often. Walking up and down the cement stairs burned off some of my fidgety energy. I was a little freaked out by the mildew and the darkness, but that didn't deter me from reveling in my independence. To this day, spiders and bugs don't really make me squirm. It's a good thing I hadn't yet entered my alien phase, though, because the boiler room would have made a great location for an extraterrestrial encounter, and it might have scared me away. We held indoor gym class there when it rained, so our dodgeball games also included avoiding the furnace. I'm not sure how long that school was used as an educational institution, but it was eventually converted into a private residence. For years after moving on from the Tolman School, however, former students referred to rest rooms as basements.

As mentioned earlier, the Tolman School only housed one first grade and one second grade class. After that, we were all sent to the big South School. It was still located within walking distance of my house, but this building contained several classes of students in each grade level, and hot lunch was served in the cafeteria. Now the stakes were higher; I was pretty nervous about preserving my smarty pants image. For this reason, the summer between second and third grade was painful for me. As my overachieving anxiety grew, I even broke out in hives the night before school started..I was trying hard not to appear high strung, so I kept my nervousness a secret. Somehow I knew that seven year olds were not supposed to experience competitive anxiety.

My mom figured the rash was poison ivy, covered me in bubble-gum colored Caladryl Lotion, and off I went. It didn't occur to me that the pink blotches might appear strange or unattractive. Mom had provided me with a way to stand out, and I jumped at the opportunity. My propensity to contract poison ivy grew as I did, and there once was a brutally itchy case that infected my hands. On that day, my ever practical mother suggested that I wear white gloves to school, so I did. They were not my short white Girl Scout parade gloves; these were the long ones worn with evening gowns. I have no idea where they came from; my mother probably saved them from her Senior Prom. Today I cringe just thinking about how ridiculous I looked. I also remember catching another little girl impersonating me. She didn't hurt my feelings, though. My self-esteem was so prominent that I just thought she was jealous.

The good news that year concerned a big change in the Sidebottom household. My mom decided it was time to go to work. A devoted mother, she wanted a full time job with mother's hours. We didn't have a second car, so her options were limited. Up until now, it had been a handy coincidence that our house was located across the street from a small independent raincoat factory. It was owned by Mr Felos and was called "Twin Kee House of Rainwear." I wonder now about the origin of that strange name, but it never seemed odd to me as a child. As a matter of fact, it was a great landmark when I became older and more social. "Across from Twin Kee's" sounded so distinguished to me. Except for a few people who confused it with the little sponge cakes filled with cream, everybody could find my house. My mom would sometimes work there a few hours a week when money was tight. My grandpa (and whatever woman he was living with at the time…more on this later) would be happy to have me visit them if I needed a babysitter. Mr Felos also gave us free raincoats from his sample section. Mine was a pretty shade of pink, and it was impressive to own a "Twin Kee" raincoat. Although the sign lasted for many years, the manufacturing center didn't. I'm sure the business fell victim to mass production and marketing. Or, maybe he just chose to retire. His daughter later turned the building into the Twin-Kee Art Studio, so the landmark remained.

As for my mother, she got herself a permanent job in my school cafeteria. *How fortunate for me. I had another shot at fame.* In my imaginative little mind, my mom was now on the same plane as the gods and goddesses who presided over our classrooms. I understood nothing about the caste system in public schools. I figured all employees were on an equal plane and admired me as much as everybody else. I was thrilled for her - hairnet, rubber soled shoes and all.

Most kids would be embarrassed to have their mom work as a lunch lady. Not Kathy Sidebottom. It took me no time at all to know each of the ladies on a first name basis, and I would strut through that lunch line like the Queen of Sheba. Those ladies would eat up my charm and courtesy, *no pun intended,* and reward me with a few extra helpings here and there. Lord knows I didn't need any extra food, but I was thrilled to be their favorite.

This is a good time to talk about food. Norma and Jack Sidebottom had grown up during the depression, and they were now raising children in the 1960's. Combine the accessibility of fresh food with the development of modern homemaking appliances, and you end up with very well-fed kids. My clothes were usually purchased on sale from the Pretty Plus section of Sears and Roebucks, and my brother's came from the Husky Boys department. Dinner at home always consisted of meat, potatoes, a yellow vegetable, a green vegetable, white Wonder bread and butter. Sometimes my mom illicitly brought home leftover American Chop Suey from the cafeteria. It was a starchy, greasy concoction of elbow macaroni, stewed tomatoes and ground beef. Yum! It would arrive, slightly congealed, in a big, clear plastic tub that had formerly held mayonnaise. Mom would add some extra tomato sauce and we'd sprinkle parmesan cheese on top. Today I grimace at the image, but it seemed like a great meal at the time. I also remember that those tubs came in mighty handy for storage once the food was gone.

As soon as we had cleaned our plates, we were rewarded with dessert. Sometimes we had jello, or fruit cocktail from the can, but most of the time my mother made homemade cakes and cookies. We were praised for our good appetites and were forbidden to leave the table without eating every bit. It wasn't usually a problem - except for the night of the lima beans.

I had never encountered such an unappealing vegetable as lima beans. I suspect they might also have come from the school cafeteria. Maybe they were a secret ingredient of luncheon loaf. In any case, they disgusted me. That night, after polishing off the rest of my dinner, those horrid beans remained on my plate. There was no place to hide them (my dog wouldn't even eat them) and my dad was not about to let me talk my way into throwing them out. Wasting food was forbidden in most post-depression families, and mine was no exception. Just like he promised, those beans were left overnight for me to eat for breakfast. Whether or not they were actually consumed, I cannot recall. If so, I've blocked that memory. Maybe my mom secretly made them disappear. Mercifully, however, Mom never served us lima beans again. As an adult, I had eaten many bowls of minestrone soup before I realized that they had made a comeback.

Although I loved school, I never appreciated gym class. I was uninterested in physical fitness. Every year during elementary school, we were weighed and measured. Patty Greene and I were always the tallest, and probably the heaviest. Unabashed, I viewed this as further evidence of greatness. Together we bonded over inactivity and a love of Hostess treats. She had three older brothers, so there were always great snacks at her house. Needless to say, I often stopped in on the way home from school. Back in those days, we knew nothing about the food pyramid or the evils of sugar. The only pyramids we knew about were the ones in Egypt, and I don't even think the President's Council on Physical Fitness had yet been created.

Since my tap dancing/figure skating/gymnastics aspirations had proven unfruitful, the walk to and from school was about all the exercise I got. While other kids were playing sports, I played dolls, teacher and piano. Admittedly, I wasn't a great pianist. The best part of practicing was that I could do it sitting down, and my mind wandered through the entire exercise. I'm not sure where our piano came from, but I bet it was handed down from one of my older cousins or some acquaintance who wanted to get rid of it. I do remember that my dad refinished it, but the stain was a strange yellowish color. We didn't have much space for a piano in our house, and it was placed quite obtrusively in the living room. That meant the whole family was subjected to my painful practice sessions. Sometimes my mom would set a timer for thirty minutes, and I admit that I wasn't above moving it forward when she wasn't looking. I took lessons from a widow who lived down the street, and she had taught my cousins before me. Every week I would arrive later and later, or try to talk our lesson away. By the time I was in seventh grade, the struggle became real, and I got busted for coming late to class and being unprepared. My parents threatened that if I was not going to practice, the piano was going away, and it did. Shortly thereafter, I recognized my passion for Broadway show tunes, and I have missed that yellow piano ever since.

Although I was a precocious, chubby drama queen, I wasn't unhappy, nor was I unpopular. A little extra weight was considered healthy during the post-depression era, so I don't remember being ridiculed. I was a great reader, a great talker, and I knew the Girl Scout Promise inside and out. Of course I wanted to be the best Girl Scout in the world, so I worked on earning extra badges in my spare time. I'm pretty sure the cooking badge was the first one. My Girl Scout leader was one of the great heroines in my life. She was liberal, artistic and a feminist before her time. The only aspect of scouting I didn't enjoy was camping. Fortunately, my parents could not afford summer Girl Scout camp. Even though I was, of course, a top cookie salesperson, *and consumer,* I had no desire to apply my cookie credit to camp. I was sure there would be hiking involved and I'd be expected to play sports. Except for that Olympic summer that I spent perfecting my gymnastic routines, I was very content to spend my vacation time reading my way to the top of the public library's summer literacy competition. If I got bored, I'd weave a few looped potholders at the South School's summer recreation program.

All American school systems of the 1960's stressed patriotism and civic pride. Most of our dads were veterans of the Korean War or World War II, and the Vietnam Conflict had not yet formally begun. My grandfather used a picture of Dwight Eisenhower as a bookmark, and pictures of JFK were displayed in some of my friends' homes. Our middle-class suburban community had lost many hometown heroes, and we were the offspring of The Greatest Generation. To promote a sense of citizenship, each of our school days started with a recitation of the Pledge of Allegiance followed by a patriotic song. Our school system employed a visiting music teacher who came to each classroom once a week with her pitch pipe and autoharp. She must have helped us learn those songs because we all knew "The Star Spangled Banner," "America the Beautiful," "Yankee Doodle" and a host of others by heart. Miss Caswell did her very best to soothe our savage beasts. *It would be breasts, but we didn't have them yet.* I always sang with gusto, just in case our music teacher had connections with Hollywood big-wigs. One year the poor woman decided to direct an elementary version of *HMS Pinafore.* I'm not sure who put her up to it, but it became her undoing. Oh how my nose was out of joint when I discovered that the main parts had gone to older students. However, I did get assigned a solo part as Cousin Hebe. It was a small consolation, but I interpreted it as recognition of my potential. I remember the time she suggested that some of us should not sing so loudly. Poor Eileen O'Brien couldn't carry a tune, so we all pointed at her and giggled. Now that I think of it, I guess she could have meant me. In any case, we had a different music teacher the next year.

The culmination of our elementary musical and patriotic training involved the annual Flag Day assembly. Since Flag Day falls on June 14th, and my birthday is June 15th, I always linked it to my birthday celebration. The event was held outside, and I don't think it ever rained on Flag Day, proving the sanctity of the ritual. Each class was appointed a special song, and we practiced for weeks. When it came time for the assembly, each grade level was assigned a designated spot on the lawn. The sixth graders had the honor of performing "The Star Spangled Banner" as the finale. For a fun twist, It was followed by a rousing "Happy Birthday Old Glory" yelled in unison by the entire crowd. *In my mind, of course, they substituted my name.* During my sixth-grade year, I decided to add an extra touch of flair to the occasion. Somehow, I managed to cajole my teacher into letting me wear the Happy Birthday crown a day early. Because I was the tallest in my class, I also got to be the Line Leader. Giddy with anticipation, I got the crazy idea that instead of assuming the usual sixth grade stroll, my class should be marching like the future leaders we were sure to become. Maybe I had worn my go-go boots to school that day and felt empowered. *Probably.* In any case, I firmly cast my hand in a salute, started calling a cadence, assumed a majorette gait and expected my fellow patriots to follow along. Nobody did, but that didn't stop me. The town photographer, who happened to be my dad's best friend, was in the right place at the right time. I made it to the front page of the Stoughton

Chronicle. There I was - the high-stepping, birthday-crowned Drum Major of the South School My poor brother was mortified. I think my parents were kind of embarrassed, too. But I, of course, considered this a career break.

It wasn't until the end of sixth grade that I reassessed my physical proportions. I remember asking my mom why, when she had two fat kids, was she always baking? She said she just wanted her family to be happy and healthy. Food was love. With puberty, however, came enhanced self-awareness, and I put all my determination into slimming down in preparation for the next big thing - Junior High. I ate many, many cucumbers that summer, and I might have even exercised a little. Between carbohydrate withdrawal and Junior High anxiety, I lost most of my pre-pubescent chubbiness. The little girl who thought entering third grade was stressful had grown into a pre-adolescent basket case as she over-dramatized the next phase of her search for greatness.

Many people, especially educators, regard the building that housed the 7th and 8th graders as a holding tank for the hormonally impaired. Kathy Sidebottom, however, was not one of them. To me, it might as well have been Emerald City, and I couldn't wait to follow the yellow brick road. The educational pedagogy of the 1970s dictated that students should be grouped according to achievement level. Incoming seventh graders were assigned to a group referred to as a division, starting with the top learners in 710. In groups of 30, students were arranged in order from overachievers to - *God Forbid* - average learners. Average divisions started at level 716 and were grouped alphabetically by last name. *What a concept.* I now had so much more to worry about. What if I found myself in a group full of average people? That would be devastating to one as star-struck as myself. All my life I had prepared to be outstanding. How would I manage to hold up my head if my brilliance wasn't recognized?

It's comforting to note that as I matured, my outlook on life became a little more practical. For example, during my elementary school years, I came to accept the hard truth that I couldn't possibly be the best at everything. It was difficult, but I learned to let some opportunities slide by, and I forced myself to make some compromises. But I still believed in the destiny of *The Chosen Baby* and I was not emotionally equipped to accept a Junior High division assignment lower than 710. My sense of competition expanded completely out of all proportion, but I never revealed the extent to which I suffered. My parents and my brother were great people, but not scholars. My mom had even advised me "Not to be too smart because boys don't like girls who know everything." I tried to comply, but I couldn't help being driven. Like my alien theory, I tried to keep most of my angst to myself. Nevertheless, it consumed my high strung conscience.

Finally, Labor Day weekend passed, and it was time to learn my Junior High fate. I'm sure I had been a restless sleeper the night before, but I masked my apprehension. I climbed on the big yellow bus and entered the portal to my future. *Did I ever mention my propensity for hyperbole?* In my mind, I had made it to the big time. Immediately I missed the smell of white paste and my lunch lady friends. I felt sad that they wouldn't see my new physique. A list on the wall contained the names of our homeroom teachers and finding my way to the "S" room was not difficult. As I entered her classroom, Mrs. Donovan, who was to serve double-duty as my math teacher, handed me my division assignment.. I breathed deeply and exhaled with glee. All my worry had been in vain - I had been assigned to division 710. My homeroom teacher commented about having a "smarty" in the room as she passed me my class schedule. Poor Mrs Donovan would soon find out that my smarts didn't apply to mathematics.

Looking back on that time, I've concluded that the Junior High experience is somewhat like giving birth. Once it's over, the pain is erased from a mother's brain. The first shock to my system involved meeting the other students on the fast-track. A few of us had been together in elementary school, but I looked into many new faces. I felt as though I had finally found my people. The year was 1970 and the learning process was highly structured. We traveled from class to class as a group, insulated against mediocrity. Looking back as an educator and a parent, I now understand the rationale behind this forced segregation. How better to control the masses and keep the hormones in suppression?

I think we took PE class with students from other divisions, but since there was no way for me to excel in a class requiring physical activity and motor skill coordination, I deemed it blessedly unimportant. Besides, the Title Nine rule providing equal rights to women's athletics did not yet exist, so PE class held no glamorous potential for stardom. Instead, the class became a horrible test of my fortitude. Unlike elementary school gym class, we were now expected to change into hideous uniforms and take showers before struggling back into our school clothes. Even worse, we had to prove we had showered. At least once a week we were required to wrap our pubescent bodies in the school issued towels, parade past the teacher and prove our cleanliness. How humiliating! As the year went on, the teacher either lost interest or gave up on monitoring our hygiene and, in lieu of showering, we all perfected the "shoulder splash" technique. A little wetness on the shoulders went a long way in providing a freshly showered appearance.

At least our locker rooms were separated by gender, and the girls had individual shower stalls. A rumor circulated that the boys all showered together. Fortunately, my imagination had a built-in wholesomeness censor, and I couldn't possibly conjure up such a perverted vision. Shower or not, we still had to struggle back into our school dresses, garter belts and nylon stockings and get to class before the next bell rang. *Yes! nylon hosiery. And we're not talking about panty hose.* Girls in my town were not allowed to wear pants to school until after 1970. We were permitted to wear knee socks instead of hose, but I could never keep mine from sagging to my ankles. Some of the skinny-legged girls kept theirs up with rubber bands, but my shins were still too chunky to make that work. Besides, being allowed to wear hosiery was a rite of passage, and most of us were quite proud to have reached that milestone. They were considered expensive, though, so most of our moms had a five-run rule. No replacement nylons until there were at least five runs.

Aside from the twice weekly humiliation of PE class, intermingling among the masses was discouraged. Our administrators tried their best to keep our potential hermetically sealed. We were even specifically assigned to a dining space in the cafeteria. Luckily, most of us were gleefully unaware of our extreme geekiness. Lest we should rest on our laurels, however, we were sternly reminded of our responsibilities as the cream of the crop, often warned against wasting our potential and cajoled into high performing academia. As thrilled as I was to be part of such an elite group, the pressure to excel was palpable. Imagine my chagrin when I discovered that I couldn't wrap my brain around algebra.

I could have been a character from *A Tale of Two Cities*. Life in Junior High truly was, "The best of times and the worst of times." It didn't take long before both Mrs. Donovan and I discovered that Kathy Sidebottom was no smarty when it came to higher mathematics. I could memorize facts and tables to beat the band, but rational and irrational numbers made no difference to me. I really wanted to be fair and like them both, but I didn't have it in me to interact with any of them. *Oh, the agony of defeat.* I wasn't wasting my potential, I just didn't have it to begin with. I struggled tremendously and agonized over my failures. Worst of all was the humbling knowledge that I wasn't perfect, and my weakness had been revealed. *The cream in my crop had curdled.*

My obsession regarding mathematical inadequacy might have quelled my quest for exceptionality had it not been replaced by one grand discovery. In a compassionate effort to make the Junior High experience more tolerable, the school administration instituted a once-weekly social event called Club Time. From the moment I first laid eyes on the mimeographed list of choices, my future obsession finally came into laser focus - Drama Club! Just as I had suspected, I wouldn't need algebraic prowess after all. My true calling was about to commence. I made my selection without faltering, circling the words in every color ink my pen case possessed. When I returned my request form to Mrs. Donovan, she nodded approvingly and told me this was the place for me. I took this as an acknowledgment of my destiny and her compassion. Apparently, my talent was obvious in even the most mundane situations, and she recognized that I was created for a fate more powerful than factoring polynomials. I almost forgave her the daily math torture and pledged to mention her in my first Academy Award acceptance speech.

The anticipation of Club Time drained my energy. I was so busy actively awaiting the commencement of my career that I couldn't concentrate on anything else. I talked about nothing but Drama Club. Some of my friends seemed quite cavalier about their Club Time choices, and I just couldn't understand that attitude. A few of them had made the same choice as me. But after listening to my overenthusiastic diatribes, I'm afraid some might have changed their minds. I viewed that as an opportunity to eliminate the competition and expand my fan base. At home, my brother informed me that Club Time was stupid and only nerds would sign up for Drama Club. This led to such histrionics on my part that all mention of Club Time was banned by my parents. And this was only the beginning ...

Finally, Club Day arrived. The first meetings were scheduled for the last period of the day. I had spent most of Tuesday afternoon planning my Drama Club outfit, and the night was spent sweetly dreaming of impending stardom. My classes that day were intolerably long, but the time finally arrived. Drama Club meetings were held in the Speech room and led by Mr Spartin, a bearded, bespeckled Thespian with a degree in Speech and Theater. Public speaking was a required class in the statewide school curriculum, providing many aspiring actors with fallback paychecks. *Of course it was one of my favorite classes. I had been waiting for an audience all my life.*

Don Spartin was a god to me. I was enraptured from the moment he walked into the room, and I held on to his every word. How fortunate it was for my family that Club Time met just once a week. As an auditory learner, I remembered every word from every meeting, and I repeated them redundantly at home. As I recall, I was a bit taken aback when Mr.Spartin mentioned auditions. I think I viewed it as a bait and switch. *Wouldn't a man of his expertise recognize talent at first glance? Why would I need to audition?* Thankfully, there had been no previous mention of auditions during the registration process. I had been adequately obsessed already. Suddenly, my energy had specific focus - I would plan the perfect audition.

While other students prepared to recite insipid nursery rhymes or Beatles' song lyrics, I created an entire skit, probably inspired by *The Carol Burnett Show.* Fortunately for everyone involved, my previous experience with live theater was limited to a few plays we saw as Girl Scouts. Had I been more culturally aware, I'm sure I would have presented a painful 7th grade version of Antigone. I'm not sure how I got them to school that day, but my presentation involved several different costume pieces and props. To the man's credit, he kept a straight face while watching the melodrama I performed, and Mr. Spartin marveled at my enthusiasm. Little did he know what a Frankenstein he was about to create.

Drama Club rescued me from the perils of public Junior High School. Although I was still determined to maintain my membership among the academic elite, I had learned to prioritize my anxiety. It didn't take me long to figure out that a grade of 91 would still earn me an "A," so I could relax a little and focus on my true passion - preparing for a life in the theater (or at the very least, a theatrical adulthood). I was completely absorbed in myself, my image and my future. As it turned out, this self-absorption was quite fortuitous. The early 1970s was a volatile time to be growing up. I was enthralled by the energy of the hippies, the war protesters, the women's rights groups and all things enhanced by the media. I didn't waste time trying to understand the political or social justice issues, I just thought they were exciting. I wasn't boy-crazy or drug-curious. Instead, I was a girl on a mission to soak up all the attention and life experience needed to become a star. Meanwhile, division 710 led to division 810. We were still harassed into working hard and reminded daily of our responsibilities, potential, and the myriad ways in which we were wasting both. Slightly scathed, with our humility high and our self-esteem falling within normal parameters, we all managed to emerge from our hormonal holding tank readily prepared to face our secondary school challenge. *Or at least that's the way I looked at it.*

In high school, I started to build my performing arts resume. Classes in chorus and drama were offered as electives, so I was as thrilled as I could be. Sometimes I faced difficulty fitting them into my rigorous academic schedule, but it all worked out in the end. I continued to be enrolled in accelerated academic classes, with the thankful exception of mathematics. I still possessed more than a healthy bit of respect for educators, and I wanted to please. Therefore, unless I drove them crazy by talking too much a*bout myself i*n class, my teachers liked me back. Every day brought another performance opportunity. I'm pretty sure that perkiness might have helped me earn a few extra points here and there, especially in the dreaded math classes.

I was relieved to be rid of the claustrophobic process of Junior High scheduling and thankful that high school offered a wider range of academic choices-especially in the math department. Admitting both relief and defeat, I took my walk of shame past my former cohorts in the honors math classes and relaxed into the regular college prep section. Once I had landed in the right place, I gladly resigned from

Fast Track Math, all privileges and frustration notwithstanding. It was time for me to broaden my horizons and jump into a bigger sea of humanity. I enjoyed meeting new people, but I didn't find college prep math any easier than Honors. Fortunately, the remaining academic classes were enjoyable. Except for the dissection part, I especially loved biology class. I had already developed great memorization skills, and I could relate each of the body systems to my favorite subject – ME. I managed to pass enough history tests to earn an A without really learning anything. Honors Freshman English was taught by a disheveled hippie-type who favored song lyric analysis. He encouraged free thought and all things liberal, and he looked a little like Rasputin. He seemed to recognize my potential as he nicknamed me Sarah Heartburn. Once, however, he scared me by saying he saw demons in my eyes and warned me that too much drama might lead to possession. I dismissed his remark, saying he had me confused with Lucy in the Sky With Diamonds. His warning, however, was never forgotten. I suspect I was not the only student who fell victim to his strange pronouncements. He was fired at the end of the year.

I glided through my freshman year with very little angst. I found my place and my people. It wasn't exactly like Riverdale or Nancy Drew's high school as I had envisioned, but there were fresh challenges, new people and my first boyfriend: a Senior. Technically, I just replaced his former girlfriend who had graduated and moved off to college, but it was another boost to my burgeoning self-esteem. My parents were not thrilled about letting me date a boy with a driver's license, but he didn't have a car of his own, so it really wasn't an insurmountable obstacle. Our dates consisted of a few Saturday afternoon movies and trips to Friendly's. In the minds of Norma and Jack, nothing bad could happen in the daytime, so they let us date. Besides, he was a drama geek, a school newspaper reporter and an honor student. They knew what that meant - pretty harmless. And he was.

The one and only time my first boyfriend and I ever pushed the envelope haunted me for years. Literally. And the worst part? I couldn't talk about it. As I mentioned before, in the Drama Room I had discovered my tribe. I quickly assumed my indisputable reign as Queen, and I was surrounded by adoring dramatic playmates. *At least that was my perception.* Referred to by some unimaginative students as Drama Fags, we were a formidable, inseparable and most enthusiastic force. We claimed a special table in the cafeteria and we had a great theater in which to hang out.

We were known to spend most of our time in wholesome pursuits except for one dangerous activity. While stumbling through adolescence during the Age of Aquarius, we discovered a new toy - a Ouija board. Could there be a more fascinating plaything for a bunch of over-dramatic teenagers? The Ouija knew everything, and we rejoiced in scaring ourselves silly. Part of the allure was the decadence involved. Consulting the Ouija was a forbidden practice in most households. In addition, since Rasputin had already planted the idea of demon possession into my brain, I was more fearful than most. Of course the drama trumped the fear, however, and I was hooked. Eventually, a Catholic parent put an end to our hi-jinks, and we surrendered our connection to the other-world. But to this day, my memory of that time struggles to differentiate reality from theatrically-induced fantasy.

At the height of our psychic furor, the most popular film of 1972 was *The Exorcist*. This is the part of the story where my boyfriend and I pushed that envelope. Every year, our drama department would participate in the annual one act play competition sponsored by The Boston Globe. Thanks to the talent and dedication of our teachers, our school presentation always made it to the state finals in Boston. Participating was the highlight of every year. Not only did we qualify for excused absence from school, but we spent a few days in the big city interacting with Drama Geeks from all over the state. Although the idea seems ludicrous by today's standards, we were also granted several hours of free, unchaperoned time. Needless to say, we took full advantage of our freedom. The top-grossing movie that year was *The Exorcist* , and it was playing at movie theaters all over Boston. No one under 18 was allowed admission, but nobody was checking id's. My boyfriend was 18, but I wasn't even close. Nevertheless, in we went. And just in case your imagination is conjuring up lewd images, let me put an end to that. We watched every minute of the movie.

Linda Blair scared the Hell out of me. I don't think I slept for a week - and certainly not without the lights on. Combined with the suggestion of demon possession, the new fantasies I harbored made my earlier alien theory seem trivial. Also, I had broken the law by sneaking in. My Girl Scout training and extreme allegiance to patriotism compounded the nature of the evil I had committed. *I was consumed with guilt.* Even worse - I suffered in silence. We didn't talk to our parents about our feelings back then, especially if we were perceived as high-strung. I was guilty, terrified, and my conscience suffered in silence. As a result, I never slept in a building alone until I was 42 years old.

To all but the most careful observer, it appeared that I had taken high school by storm. Sophomore year, however, brought a whole new unexpected obstacle - Honors Chemistry Class. I knew chemistry was going to be trouble when I first laid hands on that slide rule. I was happy to join my Fast Track friends from Honors Biology, but I was the only student who wasn't simultaneously enrolled in Honors Math. They had developed slide rule expertise, but it was a totally foreign instrument of torture to me. I commend my fellow classmates for patiently trying to catch me up, but I was totally untrainable. Between the slide rule and the inscrutable periodic table of elements, I fell farther and farther behind, so I begged both my school guidance counselor and the teacher to let me drop the class. Up until now, I had never earned a grade below a "B", and I had no coping mechanisms for academic failure. It was also clear that no amount of perky charm would work on Mr Holbert, our teacher. He was devoid of personality and/or humor. He appeared to despise me, and I wasn't used to that. His failure to appreciate my dramatic charm was puzzling. In addition, I learned that chorus class met during the same class period. Joining the chorus would lead me closer to my life goals than chemistry. In my mind, it was a lateral move. When I tried to negotiate with my guidance counselor, though, I heard those dreaded words again - "You are just not working up to your potential." Why couldn't I make them understand that my potential was waiting for me in the chorus room, not the chemistry lab? I was faced with a horrible dilemma.

Eventually the gods intervened and I found an exit. What happened next was just an accident. I didn't do it on purpose. *Honest!* I just happened to be walking past the Bunsen burners with a match. Master multi tasker that I was, a stimulating conversation was likely going on at the same time. Maybe I just wasn't paying close attention. Maybe the demons had come to possess me after all. I'm sure my fascinating story merited extensive gestures. How did I know everyone had already turned on the gas? As the jets shot flames into the air, I was banished to the chorus room and never set foot in a chemistry lab again. The alto section welcomed me with open arms, and I thanked the universe for providing such good fortune.

I loved being a member of our school chorus. After all my experiences with the academic Fast Track, it seemed delightfully decadent to sing my way through a daily class period. Although he didn't succumb to my constant requests to sing show tunes, my beloved chorus teacher did often select me as a soloist. I'm sure my singing voice wasn't as amazing as I thought - but I was always willing to be noticed. I had lung power and good pitch, and I was even compared to Ethel Merman. *I thought it was a good thing.* Looking back, I realize it was probably easier to assign me a solo than to make me blend in with the section. Our chorus was very popular in the community, and our repertoire was varied. I especially enjoyed the spring Pops Concert where the program consisted of show tunes and top 40s. These were the days of *Godspell* and *Jesus Christ Superstar*. Presenting controversial music in the 1970s was risky, but we sounded so good that nobody complained.

Mr AuClaire, our chorus teacher, worked tirelessly. Not only did he lead our award-winning chorus, but he also coached many of us for state-wide competitions. I had the honor of participating in All-State Chorus at least once during my high school career. Had there been solos involved, or another way to be singled out, I probably would have auditioned every year. Still, being part of a huge chorus was fun, and I enjoyed the status of having been selected as a member of this elite group. I still have the vinyl record that was made of our performance. The names of all participants were listed on the back in itty bitty print, but I considered it a good start toward claiming my fame.

My penance for the chemistry incident was paid during my junior year of high school. In order to meet college application requirements, I needed to take another lab science class. Most Juniors took physics, but the prerequisite to physics was chemistry. I would rather have stuck needles in my eyeballs than end up in one of Mr. Holbert's chemistry classes again, so my only recourse was an offering called Anatomy and Physiology. There was just one section offered each year, and it was especially designed for students planning careers in medicine. Of course I had no plan to become a doctor, but I thought I might play one on tv some day, so this class held potential. *Ironically, I once did play a doctor in an independent film.*

The class was taught by the charismatic Chuck Pontz, famous for his dumb jokes and puns. To this day, whenever I hear the word "urinalysis," I think "both mine and urine." He worked part-time at the BPM supermarket with my dad, and it seemed like a good fit. There was just one drawback. Anatomy and Physiology students dissected cats. (Fortunately, we didn't have to supply our own.) Instead, one day Mr. Pontz rolled out a giant bin of deceased, embalmed cats. I remember some comment about them being shipped from Italy, but I bet that was just another of his jokes.

Mr. Pontz did not give us a chance to express discomfort. One by one we rolled up our sleeves, reached in and grabbed a very stiff paw. I'm so sure there were handshake jokes involved. These cats were no small kitties, and they reeked of formaldehyde. Our first assignment was to remove the skin. *Ewwww.* We worked on these poor animals for weeks. Sometimes we even had dissection homework and carted those forty pound carcasses home. It doesn't take much imagination to picture a high school Junior bringing a trash bag full of dead cat onto a school bus. *Or maybe it does.* For me, though, it was just another way to stand out in a crowd. The dead cats weren't even carried in dark-colored trash bags. The bags were huge, heavy and transparent. Since some of my friends from the Fast Track did plan to become doctors, two of them would come over to perform cooperative surgeries in my cellar. Despite the creepiness of the situation, we always had a lot of laughs. Inhaling formaldehyde in an unventilated cellar can do that to a person. In retrospect, I came to enjoy that class and the teacher. Once we got past the cat dissection unit, it was smooth sailing.

Aside from this semi-entertaining foray into science, my greatest efforts were applied to the humanities. My imagination and communication skills were regularly recognized and rewarded in English class. (*How's that for alliteration?*) And my memorization skills served me well in Social Studies and French classes. I almost stumbled a bit when Mme Lavallee, the French teacher, recognized my last name. She asked who my mother was. Like several other teachers, she seemed surprised about the match between Jack Sidebottom and Norma Leathers I surmised that Jack had been a nice kid, but not much of a student. Even worse, Mme Lavallee had taught my mother and seemed to have adored her. I panicked. French was not my favorite subject, and I certainly didn't want her to expect more from me than I wanted to give. I immediately informed her that I was an adopted child. From then on, for four long years, she referred to me as "la petite orphane." I had no idea how many orphans there were in France, but she certainly found a great many passages for me to read.

All academic pursuits aside, my major motivation for attending school was to hone my theatrical skills. Stoughton High School students were gifted with several of the most patient teachers of the 1970s. Mr. AuClaire, the aforementioned chorus teacher, also served as the musical director of our annual musical theater presentation, and he accompanied us at each rehearsal and performance. As a Freshman, auditions for the musical *Damn Yankees* were calling my name. Since I hadn't yet set the chemistry lab on fire, I wasn't enrolled in any of his chorus classes. I'll never forget the look on his face when I walked onto that stage and belted out "I'm the Greatest Star" from *Funny Girl. Ahh, youthful arrogance.* I was told later that he and the drama teachers referred to me as premature. I almost expected to be cast in the lead role - I could have handled whatever Lola wanted - but I was cast in a supporting role as Gloria Tharpe. Needless to say, I was still very excited. My talent had been recognized, and I was going to be performing in a full-length musical on the big stage. Rehearsals were joyous endeavors, even the time when baseball players dropped me during dance rehearsal. I got to wear a cervical collar for a week. You can bet I milked that incident for all it was worth.

Another member of the performing arts team at Stoughton High School was Mrs. Deneen. The Junior High public speaking class was followed by a required High School level class, and that teaching responsibility fell onto her. Since I was one of the few students who actually enjoyed her class, I faced no competition for the position of teacher's pet. Not only was she my teacher, but we became very good friends. She had been teaching only a few years, and our ages weren't more than ten years apart. In many ways she became a mentor. In addition to collaborating with her teammates as a director, she was also the choreographer. Most cast members were as graceless as me, so that was a daunting chore. She had the added allure of being married to an actor and drama teacher from another school. They were the adults I wanted to become. Our rehearsals took place after classes were over, and as her commute to and from school brought her by my house each day, she eventually became my ride home. We enjoyed many great talks over the years. I wonder if she had ever been one of the horn-beeping fans at my Peggy Fleming Imposter skating shows? I've never thought to ask, and fortunately she never mentioned it.

The third member of the holy trinity was Dick Staff. Over the years he had built what we thought was a dramatic empire, and our sanctuary was his classroom, E205. The door to E205 seemed never to be locked. Mr Staff provided us with space and respect, often retreating to his office so he "didn't know" when we were not supposed to be there. According to us, this was where the cool people hung out. Hanging on the walls were pictures from numerous productions, and I longed to see myself on the wall. By the time I graduated, I had my own gallery. From the beginning of my Sophomore year until I graduated, I earned the leading role in almost every play. I'm sure there were some protests from other Drama Fag friends, but I turned a deaf ear. *After all, I was destined to be a star*, and I worked tirelessly toward that goal. I had the chance to play many great roles, including Winnifred in *Once Upon a Mattress* and Mame Dennis in *Mame.* My brother was vindicated by my performance as Lucy in *You're a Good Man, Charlie Brown*. That was typecasting at its best. I played some great dramatic roles as well, even receiving fan mail for my portrayal of a blind woman named Suzy in *Wait Until Dark*.

Don AuClaire, Linda Deneen and Dick Staff were everything to all of us. They tolerated noise, silliness, noise, hormones, noise, histrionics and more noise. We all adored them, and we knew it was mutual. As role models, they were impeccable. They taught us about discipline, excellence and respect for our art. In an era of turbulence, they provided a secure cocoon. My parents were among many, I'm sure, who marveled at the wholesome quality of our teenaged lives. As we used to say, drugs and alcohol were not needed. We were "high on life."

Many of us have remained friends for decades, and we revel in the drama of our grown up lives. In the 1990s, a friend who had fine-tuned the art of stage management during her high school days started organizing reunions. She did her best to track down all performing arts participants from the decade of the 70s. That was no small feat, but she loved the idea of organizing a reunion. Many of us traveled back home to pay tribute to those amazing years. The teachers we regarded as the The Holy Trinity were all in attendance, as were their spouses. We celebrated a meeting of the mutual admiration society. What fun it was to share a glass of wine with our former teachers. It felt delightfully decadent. We met every other year for six years. Sadly, we lost both our organizer, Elaine, and Mr AuClaire to strokes. We stopped formally meeting, but Facebook keeps us connected. Dick Staff and Linda Deneen are still cheering us on. As a matter of fact I recently sent Dick Staff a chapter of this book. He is the father of an adopted child, and

I knew he would get a kick out of the drama that was still part of my life. All three teachers encouraged me to pursue a career in performing arts, which I did. They were my cheerleaders when I auditioned for undergraduate programs in theater, and they inspired me to pursue a master's degree in education. They were flattered that I was following in their footsteps. For many years I heard their words in my voice as I led my noisy young thespians toward fulfilling their potential, and I hope I made them proud.

To say that my childhood was full of support and wholesomeness would be an understatement. I'm grateful and still a little bit amazed by my good fortune. Sometimes I feel guilty and wonder how I deserved such an idyllic upbringing. I wasn't the easiest kid to raise. The budding drama queen my parents adopted didn't adhere to the modest, unassuming norms they had expected. My craving for attention demanded stamina, but their supply was never exhausted. Now that I'm a mother and a teacher, I know there were times when my antics must have driven them crazy. Yet, with the help of their support system, they persevered. I love them for who they were, and who they raised me to be.

Part Two
My Adoptive Heritage

A ll of the clichés ascribed to members of the Greatest Generation apply to my adoptive parents, Norma and Jack Sidebottom: salt of the earth, pillars of the community, humble and kind. They were representative of good Yankee stock. Norma was the second child born to William Harold and Cora Mae Leathers. William and Cora were both from the great state of Maine, and they were cousins. I must say that this detail seemed odd to me - especially when I learned about chromosomes in biology class. I was told by my mother, however, that they were second cousins, and the custom wasn't unusual back then, especially in small New England towns where the matrimonial pickings were slim. *In any case, she and her brother seemed to be okay, so I'll just leave it alone.* Norma Elizabeth (or Norma Betty as she liked to be called) was a cheerful child, born on December 26, 1926, and raised in a tiny house on Broadway Street in Stoughton. (The reference to Broadway mustn't be overlooked. I took that as another sign of my destiny.) As a matter of fact, every visit to my grandparents could be considered a performance opportunity.

It saddened me that my mom's birthday fell on the day after Christmas. It just didn't seem fair. My June birthday was perfect - I got presents every half year. I always tried to make it up to her. I insisted that her birthday should not be celebrated as a 2 for 1 Christmas event. She deserved a day of her own. Norma, however, thought it was great to be able to share her special day with a holiday. That's the kind of person she was, always making the best out of a situation.

The modest home where she and her brother grew up was within walking distance of the First Parish Unitarian Church in Stoughton square, and Norma was a lifelong member. During her childhood, the congregation was large. I was told later that for many years, people attended that church more for its proximity to the center of town than for its teachings. Norma, however, was a devoted Unitarian and a lifelong member of this liberal faith. In her senior years, she was adored by all parishioners as one of their sacred elders. I heard an anecdote about an incident involving my mom during a Children's Sunday service a few years ago. The minister asked everybody who attended Sunday school to come forward to receive a special balloon. To the surprise and delight of the entire congregation, up walked 90 year-old Norma. Relishing her role as the oldest Sunday School graduate, she happily accepted her balloon, wrapped the string around her cane and quietly returned to her seat. She got spunky in her later years. Mom had a great sense of humor, but it was usually shared in a more understated manner. It took her sixty years, but I like to think some of my theatrical flair finally rubbed off on her.

By the time my brother and I were enrolled in Sunday School, the Unitarians had merged with the Universalists and elongated the name. Being a UU became a tough gig. Not only was it an odd-sounding religion, but most of the people who came to settle in our growing neighborhoods were Catholic. By the 1960's, the town of Stoughton, Massachusetts, had developed into a bedroom community for Boston commuters. Large companies like IBM and Raytheon brought well-paying jobs for white collar workers, public rail transportation was readily available, and the population increased greatly. In addition, the town welcomed a large influx of Portuguese-American citizens who were devout Catholics. Two Catholic churches and a parochial school were built to accommodate the newcomers. I, of course, envied what I perceived to be the drama of Catholic Liturgy. Wearing hats to church seemed like a great costuming opportunity. On Saturday afternoons I often accompanied one friend or another to confession. My imagination wildly visualized the inside of a confessional, and I wished I had been allowed to participate. I would have traded my LRY (Liberal Religious Youth) meetings for a First Holy Communion ceremony any day. Unitarian Universalism sounded exotic, but I was somewhat dismayed by its lack of glamour.

As I mentioned before, both Jack and Norma grew up during the Depression years. The stories they told of their childhood, however, made the era sound far less than depressing. But then again, both of my parents were consummate optimists. I know from studying history that the times were stressful and the economy bleak. What I heard about Norma's childhood, though, exuded positive nostalgia. It was filled with laughter, friends and humble pursuits. Her best friend, Pauline Govey, lived right across the yard, and I envisioned a tin-can and string telephone connecting their homes. They remained close companions until she passed away a few years before my mom. Pauline eventually suffered from Alzheimer's disease, but my mother visited her often and discovered that singing songs from the 1940s would create moments of lucidity. I easily picture them sipping lemonade and singing "Don't Sit Under the Apple Tree" in wavering voices. That image captures not only the resourcefulness, but also the sweetness of my mother's nature.

Pauline's husband, John Ceruti, was a mailman, and he kept close tabs on most of the townies - their friends since high school. The Cerutis had two daughters who grew up to become babysitters for my brother and me, and later Pauline had what my mother called a second family - two sons whom I would babysit while their parents were out with the bowling league. I love the sense of symmetry that connected their lives.

In her reminiscence, my mother made it seem that kids those days lived very simple lives. They were required to find their own entertainment without parental intervention or interference. In many ways it seemed as if the Depression leveled the playing field. I was led to believe that people didn't focus on status back then, and cooperation overruled competition. I believed in *Leave it to Beaver.* My mom's youth sounded like a never-ending game of kick the can.

At my mother's funeral, she was repeatedly described as nice. This is simple and true; she was the nicest person I ever knew. I attribute part of her sweet nature to genetics and part to her spirituality. Although she loved me unconditionally, I know she struggled to comprehend my fierce drive and competitive nature. On more than one occasion I was advised that life was too short to be spent worrying, so I know she acknowledged my anxious nature. In reference to my competitiveness, it made her sad to think that I might not grow up to be as nice as she was. For example, when I was a teenager, "mean girls" were very much part of the culture. *I'm pretty sure I was one myself, although I was too much of a geek to be part of the popular crowd.* Norma never liked hearing my girlfriends and me gossiping about other girls, and I was the recipient of more than one lecture about how "everybody got along when I was a kid." Her youth sounded as idyllic as a scene from the play *Our Town*.

Although my mother had no sister, she was extremely close to her first cousin, Connie. Connie grew up about four hours away in Maine, and my mother often said they were as close as sisters. I'm amazed at their ability to maintain a strong and consistent relationship with so little opportunity to connect. In those days, of course, even telephone conversations were impossible. The strong bond between them is a tribute to the family's sense of loyalty. Also, a simpler life meant fewer distractions, and the focus on friends and family was paramount. Friendships were fewer in number, but greater in depth. The cousins participated in summer visits and family reunions as frequently as possible, and that was enough to cement the bond of their friendship. According to Norma, Connie had always been determined to flee the state of Maine and live a sophisticated life. But these plans were abandoned when she met Richard Ireland. Richard was a humble dairy farmer and Connie became a hard-working farmer's wife. Together they ran a dairy farm near Waterville, Maine. They raised five children and many, many cows. Sometimes they would add pigs to their collection. I think I stopped eating bacon the year that Arnold appeared on the breakfast table. During one of our annual visits, Connie served us a huge breakfast of eggs, toast and some bacon she referred to as "Arnold". Arnold was not only the name of the pig raised for slaughter, but it was also the name of Connie's father, who was still alive and vibrant. I was disturbed by this choice of nomenclature, especially when it seemed the pig's fate was predetermined. I was raised to be polite, however, so I kept my comments to myself and stuck to eating just eggs and toast.

As kids, my brother John and I spent time every summer visiting the farm. The drive between our home in Massachusetts and the Ireland homestead in Albion, Maine was about three and one-half hours. You would think the journey lasted for days. Every year my father would carefully consult his AAA triptik and determined the halfway point to be the Portsmouth, New Hampshire rotary. There, the allure of Howard Johnson's clean restrooms awaited us. Sometimes my mother packed us lunch, and we would eat it at one of Hojo's outside picnic tables. If my parents' finances were flush that year, we were allowed an ice cream cone for dessert. Howard Johnson's was famous for offering 28 flavors of ice cream, and I still crave the shaved slivers of semi-sweet chocolate used in their mint chocolate chip.

My brother and I would argue and fight our way through most of the trip. Fortunately, seat belts were not required in the 1960's, so we had no weapons. Air conditioning was also non-existent, and for some unknown reason my father would celebrate the trip by smoking a cigar. This was something he did only on the way to Maine. As an adult, I have often pondered this aberrant behavior. I wonder if he was making some kind of a statement? As I grew older, I realized how ill at ease my father must have been on the farm. The work there was endless, and I'm not sure he had much in common with Richard the farmer. *This is the way he used his vacation time?* Maybe he didn't really enjoy being there, and he was bolstering his self-control? This yearly trip was important to my mother, however, and his devotion to her was unquestionable, so it became a tradition.

I was personally responsible for making the trip unpleasant in yet another way - there was always a better than even chance that I would get carsick. We kept a bucket in the back seat just for such an occasion. Jack was always appreciative of the scenery we'd pass on our interstate trips, and he didn't want us to miss a bit of it. There was just one problem. In his enthusiasm to point out the sights, he tended to veer off toward the side of the road, and then over-correct. In other words, he was a swerver. To make matters worse, hitting the brake was an action reserved as a last resort. I was the mother of two children before I realized that the true cause of my carsickness was the combination of stinky cigar smoke and my father's jerky driving. Even as an adult, the condition would return whenever I rode in the back seat of my father's car.

The carsickness scenario was always the same: once I grew tired of bickering and decided to ignore my brother, *and subliminally irritate my father, I'm sure,* I would stick my nose in a book. This combination wreaked havoc within my stomach. Anticipating my father's frustrated response, I always waited until the last minute to announce the need to pull over. If I had just provided more warning time, the situation would have been less dramatic, but not as traumatic. But such an option never crossed my mind. The optimist within me always hoped the nausea would pass, but it never did. Sooner or later the wave would overcome me. Jack would be annoyed, John often got hit with errant vomit, and Norma always wondered why my tummy failed to provide a warning. As compensation, I got to eat saltine crackers for the rest of the ride. Fortunately, by the time I hit Junior High, my riding habits slightly improved. I credited my Drama Club training. Embracing the concept of dramatic timing made the trips improve. I still got carsick, but at least I learned to provide ample warning.

Once we arrived at the farm, John was in his happy place. My brother was a great help and he loved every aspect of farm life. As a matter of fact, John went on to graduate from Norfolk County Agricultural High School and attended Essex County Agricultural

College. He would have loved to have had a farm of his own, but that opportunity never materialized for him. Once he became a teenager, he would take a bus up to Maine early in the summer and work with his cousins for weeks.

I, on the other hand, tried to stay as far away from the barn as possible. My role was to provide comic relief. Our arrival provided a brief respite period for the ladies of the house. Connie still bore the responsibility of cooking enormous meals for her family and a few day laborers, but my brother happily assumed her early morning and evening milking shifts. My mom would help with the cooking and the endless household chores. I'm not really sure what my dad was doing - I find it hard to believe he would be very useful in the barn, but I bet they had home repair projects to keep him occupied. As for me, I was the summer diversion for my cousins Laurie and Holly. We laughed and laughed and played endless games of Monopoly. Since we never wanted to make each other lose, we just kept lending each other Monopoly money. The game would consume our days, and we spent our evenings chasing lightning bugs. Sometimes, if the schedule allowed, we would pile in the back of the pickup truck and take a swim in China Lake. It was a special treat for everyone...except me.

China Lake was the muddiest swim hole I ever encountered. *Granted, my aversion to physical exercise prevented encounters with swim holes in general, but still...* Next to the splintery dock were raw hunks of Styrofoam to use as floats. I could have balanced on them to avoid touching the bottom, but they irritated the fat rolls on my belly. The alternative was to sink to my shins in mud. In retrospect, I'm thankful that my parents raised me to be polite. This was a horrible experience, but I conjured up enough acting ability to make the best of the situation. I viewed it as an opportunity to stockpile reserves of fortitude needed for my future. I hoped to apply my discomfort to a future acting exercise. As much as I loved my cousins, the summer visits confirmed my commitment to a more glamorous future lifestyle. Unless offered a role on an episode of *Green Acres,* rural life held no appeal for me. Nevertheless, Norma and Jack believed in raising well-rounded children, and our exposure to rural life was viewed as a major contribution toward our enrichment.

Aside from Connie and her family, Norma had no other immediate family members. Sadly, World War II brought tragedy to Norma's life when her only brother Earle was killed in Normandy. She rarely spoke of him, but when she did it was with a sense of patriotic resignation. Once in a while she would reminisce about his sense of humor and tell us how much he would have enjoyed knowing my brother and me, but her tone was never maudlin. My brother was named John Earle in memory of him, and she kept his official Army photograph on her dresser throughout her entire adult life. The resemblance among she, him and their father was remarkable. The picture was one of those black and white photographs that had been colorized by hand, so Earle's cheeks contained a permanent rosy glow.

Every time the seasons changed, Norma would take us to visit the local cemetery, stoically caring for the perennials that decorated Earle's commemorative marker. No tears were ever shed as we also decorated graves of relatives I never heard about. Public displays of emotion were not part of the tradition. This was typical behavior regarding most of her past. Whatever painful emotions she felt were maintained internally. She lived in the present, always grateful and looking ahead. I'm sure this is another reason why I was reticent to express my recurrent bouts of anxiety. Subliminally I was taught that it was counterproductive.

Several years after Earle's death, Norma was faced with another major challenge when she contracted tuberculosis. Again, I don't know much about this time in her life because it was seldom mentioned, and I never thought to ask. Here is another example that illustrates the overtly positive nature of her personality and her refusal to dwell on the past. The first I remember hearing about her experience with tuberculosis was when she briefly mentioned a stay at a sanitarium. I must have been a teenager because I immediately fantasized about her mental status. I must have responded dramatically, because Norma immediately recognized her semantic error and switched the word to "sanatorium." Tuberculosis in the 1940s was fairly prevalent, and she became one of its victims. I assume she responded quickly to treatment. It is quite possible that her bout with the illness was responsible for the infertility she and Jack later faced. My brother and I never really knew for sure because it was never offered up as a subject for discussion. My parents believed in the value of personal privacy. For her, it was just another obstacle to overcome. Maybe in her scorebook of unpleasant experiences, tuberculosis recovery wasn't as traumatic an event as surviving the Depression or losing her brother in World War II.

Herein lies a major character difference between my mother and me. Had I lived through a medical crisis like tuberculosis, I doubt I'd be able to dismiss it as easily. At some point I certainly would have constructed an emotional monologue detailing every aspect of treatment, willingly sharing it with anyone who expressed interest. My personality is extroverted, and my coping skills involve talk therapy. (I'm not saying this is a good thing) To my mom, however, the desire to preserve personal privacy superseded her need for attention or sympathy. She didn't like to share unpleasant news; I would never have given it a second thought.

In addition to being the nicest person I ever knew, my mom was also the strongest. Norma survived three battles with cancer, and she credits her recovery to the power of positive thinking. Her first bout with cancer involved melanoma. A large tumor was removed from her leg, and she enjoyed twenty years of remission before she was diagnosed with Non-Hodgkins Lymphoma. By this time, Norma was in her seventies, but she faced the challenges of chemotherapy and radiation with her usual optimism. In addition to standard medicine, she also embraced the practices of self-hypnosis, visualization, and Reiki. My daughters and I jokingly referred to her as "New Age Nana", but I'm sure her experiences later inspired her granddaughters' decision to pursue a Master's Degree in Positive Psychology. Even when the cancer diagnosis reached Stage Four, her indomitable spirit beat the odds. Five years later, she beat breast cancer. Although I know he was terrified, my Dad's support was always there - solid as a rock

It may seem ironic that seven years later, my father died of lung cancer. He had never been sick in his life, and my mother's strength was put to the test again as she assumed the role of his caretaker. His cancer progressed quickly, and his experience was emotionally heart-wrenching. I believe this is the true reason why she survived - in order to ease my father's passing."This," she told me once, "is the secret to a good marriage - we take care of each other."

Sharing, and taking care of others was always part of my mother's life. It was how she was raised. She told me that while she was growing up , my grandparents often invited other people to live with them. As my mother said, they "took people in". I don't know where these people slept. There was very little space, food or privacy, but they all seemed to manage just fine. The visitors were usually described as aunts or cousins, but the genealogy always seemed a bit sketchy. I think the title Aunt (rhyming with want) was used loosely in reference to any single older woman. When I was growing up I referred to several elderly women as aunts, but I'm not even sure my mother could explain the genetic connection. I guess it was a Yankee tradition.

Sadly, my maternal grandmother died from cancer when I was about five years old, so I have few memories of her. After she passed, some of the aforementioned aunts came to live with Grandpa. They were very sweet, and I guess they were there to keep house, even though Grandpa had retired from his job at the leather factory and appeared to be quite self-sufficient. Ironically, my Grandpa, William Harold Leathers, worked in a leather factory. Sometimes Aunt Ida lived in Grandpa's house, and sometimes the housemate was Aunt Edna. Both were shipped down on the train from Maine in flowered house dresses and black sensible-heeled shoes. They both smelled like sweet talcum powder and wore circle pins on the left side of their ample breasts. They never came together, just one or the other. I guess they took turns as a tag team. I think one of them might have been Grandpa's sister, and one was Nana's sister, but I'm really not sure. I am sure, however, that both were determined to preserve Yankee traditions, including the frying of homemade donuts on Saturday mornings.

Those donuts were epic. As soon as they were fried crispy and brown, each one ended up in a paper bag full of sugar waiting to be shaken. On special occasions, cinnamon would be added, or they might be shaped into crullers. Nothing tasted as good as those greasy, sugary confections. My brother and I would conjure up all kinds of excuses to be at Grandpa's house on Saturday morning. This time in our lives preceded the invasion of Dunkin' Donuts throughout Massachusetts, and even those Kings of Confection couldn't replicate the home-made donut experience. *If I have initiated a craving, I apologize. If I have, and it needs to be satisfied, I have a suggestion. I have discovered that a plain Dunkin' Donut placed for 10 seconds in a microwave comes pretty close to rendering satisfaction.*

Not all of the Aunt's traditions were as well received as the donuts. One example is a peculiar incident involving dandelions. One day I picked a bouquet of dandelions for one of the Aunts. I'm not taking credit for initiating this random act of kindness. I suspect that Chatty Kathy might have been sent outside to give Aunt Whomever's ears a rest, and I made the best of the situation. Imagine my surprise when I later discovered my flowers boiling in a pot on the stove. Seldom was I ever a quiet child, but I was suddenly stunned me into silence. At my tender age I hadn't yet encountered the concepts of homeopathic cures or voodoo, but I knew about witches. I was scared to death, and with good reason. I knew that Norma's family complemented their Universalist-Unitarian beliefs with some practices from the Spiritualist Church. Conjuring spirits from beyond and tipping tables was within my grandparents' realm of entertainment. Sometimes my mom's cousin Connie would mention ghosts or spirits who played tricks on her at the farm. As might be expected, those boiling dandelions got my imagination going in all kinds of directions. I was afraid to ask about them, but I had lots of suspicions. Once again I was thankful to have been brought up as an obedient child who kept her suspicions to herself, and I did. But obviously the incident remained stuck in my brain.

Many years later, as an adult, I do remember once discussing my grandfather's living arrangements with my mother. "Didn't you think it was a little weird?" I asked her. She replied, "No, I never thought about it." This meant, of course, that I shouldn't either. I guess it was just another one of those old Yankee customs. I will say my grandfather was great company, so maybe the Aunts just conjured up an image of his helplessness to get out of Maine for a while. I'm sure that's something I would have done.

The greatest legacy left by Norma's family was an uncanny sense of humor and imagination. I cannot begin to count the number of times my mom would utter some witticism prefaced by "My mother used to say..." Some of her statements would make sense, such as, "Make hay while the sun shines," but others were just plain goofy, like "Whistling girls and cackling hens often come to some bad ends." That little ditty was most likely uttered in response to an inordinate amount of whistling on my part. I'm sure it's not surprising that I tended to be obsessive in my attempts to acquire new performance skills. My mom was probably trying to make it stop...in a nice way.

It is unfortunate that my Nana Leathers passed away before I got to know her well. Judging from my mother's endless supply of quotes, she sure seemed to have had a lot to say. Perhaps therein lies the origin of my loquaciousness. I'm sure I loved chatting with Nana while I could. Grandpa, however, was my first best friend. Known for his outgoing personality and good humor, he enjoyed talking my brother and I into doing the craziest things. For example, if we were riding in the car and went over a bridge, we had to hold our noses and put our heads in our laps. John and I did it, every time, without ever questioning why. He also convinced my brother and me that the banging of the furnace pipes in his house was being done by "Peter," a guy who lived in the basement. This made as much sense to us as the Easter Bunny and Santa Claus, and we accepted it as truth. The house was old and very creaky, so Peter was a busy guy. On a heavier note, sometimes, while my parents enjoyed a night out with their friends, we would have sleepovers at Grandpa's house. One night he told me that the spirit of my Nana might come visit and knock on my walls. He'd say those kinds of things in a matter-of-fact manner, and I'm sure the statements were made in the spirit of authentic kindness. Although I never mentioned it to anyone, he had no idea how much that frightened me. For many years I thought this was normal behavior for all families. Didn't everybody experience nocturnal visitations from deceased loved ones? No wonder I grew up thinking I was an alien.

My Grandpa (and whatever Aunt was currently in residence) served as our emergency contact at school. On rare sick days, I would lounge on the couch sipping flat ginger ale and nibbling on crackers. They never tasted as good at any other time or place. My brother and I revelled in our roles as his only grandchildren. We both adored Grandpa, and the feeling was mutual. Never would we be mollycoddled or spoiled, but Grandpa paid us lots of attention, and his patience was endless. My favorite memories include reading books to him way before I knew what the words said and performing ballet recitals without ever having taken a lesson. I bet I resembled one of those dancing hippos from Disney's *Fantasia.* Fortunately, Grandpa possessed an amazing ability to keep a straight face. During the 1960s the virtue of humility was prized above self-confidence, but

Grandpa was an accomplice in my quest for stardom. When in his presence, I was the center of the universe.

I was about twelve years old when my Grandpa passed away from Parkinson's disease. For many years I thought of him as my Guardian Angel. I knew he watched all my high school performances from the spirit world, and I always sent him a little prayer before I stepped on the stage. He was my silent cheerleader. I thank him for passing his generous, kind spirit and sense of humor on to his daughter and, hopefully, to me.

There was another member of my mother's family who deserves mention. His name was Clarence. Norma referred to him as a cousin, but I have no idea how that lineage played itself out. My mother had never been able to adequately explain. He was quite a bit older than Norma, and he had been one of the people who lived with her family on and off during the Depression years. I know very few facts about him except that he survived long into his 80s, and he outlived two wives and both of my grandparents. There were stepchildren, and he had no biological children of his own. During his declining years, Norma and Jack served as loyal caretakers to this mysterious relative. He would be a silent guest at the Thanksgiving dinner table, circling back for Christmas. I don't think he ever even asked anyone to pass the salt. Clarence owned a house in a neighboring town, and my parents made it possible for him to live in his home until the day he died.

According to Norma, Clarence sometimes had "spells," and Jack would drive over, pick him up and "take him in." He would stay at my parents' house until the episode passed. He was a taciturn Yankee, so I don't remember ever engaging in much conversation with him. He wasn't unpleasant - I guess his goal was to be as unobtrusive as possible. He followed a regular routine during his overnight stays. Shortly into the evening, he would begin his ascent up the stairs to the spare bedroom with an announcement that "if he was alive in the morning, he'd see us then." He always was, and we always did. When he was living at his own house, Norma would frequently call to check on him. She and Jack would set up periodic lunch dates with him and his girlfriend, and I'm sure Clarence enjoyed their company.

Shortly after Clarence peacefully passed away at home, Norma learned that she was the sole beneficiary of his will. A bit of awkwardness among distant relatives and step-relatives ensued, but the law was final. She discovered that Clarence had spent most of his life planning to repay the kindness of his relatives. He had purchased a savings bond every year of his life, and most had reached maturity. He also owned his own home and car. He had bequeathed to her a significant amount of money. Like everything else, however, the inheritance was met with modesty and dignity. They made no significant lifestyle changes, not even adding a downstairs bathroom or moving the laundry facilities out of the cellar. Norma claimed that climbing the thirteen steep stairs to the only bathroom, or descending the twelve stairs to the laundry facilities in the cellar kept her young, and she remained in our family home well after Jack passed away. They were somewhat embarrassed by the inheritance and didn't want to appear "showy" to their lifelong friends. And, as always, my parents' first priority was their family. John and I were presented with monetary gifts intended to help pay off some bills. The oldest grandchild was given Clarence's used car. My parents pledged to help each of the other five grandchildren acquire a used car when the appropriate time arrived, and of course they did.

Norma's inheritance was the answer to my parents' prayers. Jack had been very nervous about retirement finances, and he could now relax. They had always enjoyed traveling, but their budget was tight. Now they were able to visit several places in Europe, including a trip to Normandy to pay homage to Earle. By that time, my husband's employer had relocated us to Atlanta, and visiting their Southern grandchildren no longer presented a hardship. Eventually their sixty year-old house was covered with vinyl siding and a garage door opener was installed. Those were their most extravagant purchases. It is comforting to know that the kindness inherent in the Leathers family did not go unrewarded, and I am pleased that my parents' retirement years were stress free.

As Norma's upbringing had been quiet and simple, Jack's was louder and more complicated. My dad's family was also from the town of Stoughton, but they were a much larger, more boisterous group. Jack was the second son and fourth child born to a family of five children. His father's father had come to America from England on a Clipper ship, and I grew up hearing a rumor that my grandmother descended from an American Indian Princess. *Perhaps that was the origin of my delusions of grandeur?*

The age span between the first Sidebottom baby and the final was at least 20 years. The first three, Bernice, Olive and Alfred were close in age, as were the last two, Jack and Ruth. In addition, Jack's family raised several foster children and one, Richard, lived with them during most of his childhood. They were an active, industrious family, also deeply steeped in Yankee tradition.

One would think the name "Sidebottom" held an interesting etymology, but the truth is pretty disappointing. After extensive research, one of my cousins discovered that the name originated in England with a man who lived at the side of a hill near the bottom. I spent some time thinking about that poor man. How could that be his only distinguishing quality? *How sadly ordinary.* Here was some DNA I was happy NOT to have inherited. This pitiful situation, however, served to further fuel my ambition. I owed it to that far-away ancestor to make that name distinctive.

Jack's parents chose names for their children based on ancestry. Some names are common, and some sound quite British. My father was John Osgood, and his siblings were Ruth Arline, Alfred Oland, Olive Louise and Bernice Elizabeth. Bernice was the oldest, and she inherited her mother's first name. In turn, she handed the name down to her daughter. In a gesture of compassion, Bernice III (Bunny) loosened the chain and named her daughter Holly Bernice. I think that's a good compromise. My Nana Sidebottom, Bernice I, lived to see her 90s and my aunt, Bernice

II, passed at the age of 106. Bernice III and Holly Bernice are still going strong. Longevity, small stature and boundless energy were all linked to the name.

From needlework to hospitality to childcare, generations of Sidebottom girls were masters of multitasking. As adults they shared the goal of preserving family tradition. One example is the hand knit Christmas stocking created for each baby or newlywed (and sometimes pet) who enters the family. The original ones were made of heavy wool, but now they are knitted in stretchier acrylic yarn. (That means they hold more treasures) They are each personalized at the top, and the pattern features a snowman with multi-colored building blocks. I doubt anyone has kept a tally of how many have been made, but the tradition is now in its fifth generation. When I became a grandmother, I personally tried to make one for my sweet grandson, Jack. My Aunt Ruth got me off to a great start, but my final product turned out to be quite oddly shaped. I've saved it for him as evidence of his Granna's determined effort. If anything, it has provided a few laughs. In the meantime, he inherited the original stocking made for his great-grandfather who is also his namesake. Needle-craft skill is officially recognized as another trait I did not inherit, but it doesn't stop me from trying.

Like the Leathers family, the Sidebottoms prized self-discipline, hard work and patriotism. They, too, managed to survive the Depression with even more mouths to feed. World War II greatly impacted the Sidebottom family, too, but all of their soldiers returned home. Since his big brother had joined the

Navy, Jack enlisted as soon as he could. Like many young men of that era, he was promptly shipped off to sea. Both his 18th birthday and high school graduation occurred three days after he set sail. Although I'm sure he was terrified, he spoke of that time with reverence.

There was no shortage of family pride as the Sidebottom sisters eagerly supported the war effort. My older cousins received dolls and toys from all the foreign countries their uncles visited. Letters written back and forth from family members still exist, and my brother John has possession of my dad's sea trunk. Years after the war, Jack would occasionally pull out the trunk and show us the contents. For many years, he drew the curtains so no passers-by would see the Japanese flag he managed to procure. I'm not sure if he had stolen it in Japan, or he still feared his enemies, but that flag was never displayed in public.

Jack served on the ship USS Enoree, and he was thrilled when shipmates reunited fifty years after the war. I like to think I played a small part in making that happen. When my husband's job moved us to Atlanta in 1993, my dad realized that his best Navy buddy lived within twenty miles of our house. He and my mom had the opportunity to meet up with Burt and his wife every time they visited, and they eventually created a network of contacts. A reunion committee was formed, and yearly events were held in various parts of the country. My parents came to count those annual reunion trips among their favorite memories. The Navy wives hit it off so strongly that my mother attended two reunions even after my father had passed away.

As in many towns across the country, the Stoughton, Massachusetts, chapter of the VFW maintains small squares of land named after war veterans. I'm proud to say that the efforts of both my father and my uncle Earle are memorialized in such squares. What an honor it is to see a sign bearing your loved one's name as a public acknowledgment of his service and/or sacrifice. My father's square was dedicated posthumously, two years after he died of cancer, but my brother, mother and I held proud memories of the dedication ceremony. I feel proud of my adoptive heritage every time I pass the sign, *even if the name on the sign is Sidebottom!*

My Nana Sidebottom told me that Jack had been a sickly baby, and that he looked just like a monkey. I'm sure he appreciated that. It's hard to believe that he grew into the handsome young man shown in his official Navy photo. By the time I was added to the family, Nana and Grampie Sidebottom had acquired fourteen grandchildren and a bunch of great-grandchildren. Grampie was a very tall, stern man of few words, but his dedication to family and service were clear. By the time I came along, they had been married for almost least fifty years. I can tell by looking at the Golden Anniversary pictures that I was at least two years old because I had a full head of hair. My older cousins tell me that Nana was quite strict when they were growing up, but she was nothing but fun and indulgent with me. She would have been in her seventies, and I was her last granddaughter, so I guess she was ready to do some spoiling.

During their retirement years, my grandparents spent summers living in a trailer on Cape Cod. One day a week would be Nana's Goodie Cooking Day, and the spare bed was topped with dish towels and spread with cookies. At the conclusion of every visit with Nana, the grandchildren and great-grandchildren (some close to my age) would fill bags to take home. That's how she became Goodie Nana. She taught me to knit, crochet and spend my time wisely. Although I was never an expert at needlecraft, my time management skills are excellent. She once told me that I wasn't a fat child, just "portly," and that my dramatic talent came from the elocution lessons she took as a child. *Obviously the Sidebottom family had their own brand of imagination.*

Nana and Grampie always kept busy, as did any family members within their proximity. This was not a family who chilled. Sidebottoms were huge proponents of DIY long before it was a trendy acronym. I swear that some projects were undertaken just for the opportunity to do something with their hands. The only time I ever remember being fussed at by my grandmother was when I uttered a pre-adolescent pronouncement of ennui. She cured that condition right away. The next thing I knew, I had knitted a pot holder. Boredom had no place in the life of a Sidebottom, and Dad eagerly manifested Nana's attitude. He was one of those people who required less sleep than usual, and he needed to be kept busy. He energetically took on projects of home improvement and repair, much to Norma's delight. In her mind, Jack was capable of making anything work. It wasn't until I became an adult and developed a more discerning eye that I learned the truth. Although Jack was pretty good at fixing things, sometimes his efforts didn't turn out quite right. *Not unlike grandson Jack's hand-knit Christmas stocking.* Pride and effort, however, trumped perfection. As children, we were trained not to look too closely.

My father's youngest sister, Aunt Ruth, was especially close to my grandparents. Her husband and his brothers owned a well-drilling business that operated on Cape Cod in the summer and in Jupiter, Florida in the winter. Toward the end of August, Aunt Ruth, Uncle Paul and my three cousins would pack up and move to Florida for the school year. As they got older, Nana and Grampie were encouraged to join them for the winter. I was devastated to see my grandparents leave for Florida, but mostly I was jealous to think that my cousin Cindy would have more time with Nana than I would. Cindy was just a few years older than me, and even within my family, my competitive personality knew no boundaries. Fortunately for me, that phase of their lives only lasted a few years.

Toward the end of their lives, Nana and Grampie moved into the new Senior Citizen housing development in Stoughton. I believe they were one of the first couples to take advantage of the new subsidized apartments created for the elderly. Both of them were blessed with excellent health and the longevity gene locked into their DNA. Every day, Grampie would take a walk around the neighborhood to, as he said, "Check on the widows." I can't imagine that the visit involved much conversation, but he was handy and could always be counted on to change a lightbulb. It also provided him with an opportunity to walk off some of that endless Sidebottom energy. He lived well into his 80s, and his passing left Nana alone for ten more years. I'm sure she missed him, but she wouldn't have wasted much time grieving. Sidebottoms are never bored or lonely, and her lifelong habits ensured she stayed productive. Two of her five children lived close by, and my brother and I made frequent visits. I would sometimes walk from the Junior High or High School to pay her an afternoon visit. As long as her eyesight lasted, there would be a needlework project in the works. When I was younger, we loved to cut out pictures from magazines and make scrapbooks. She used to order monthly Pak-O-Fun kits which contained all the pieces and directions needed to create a craft. Hands were never idle at Nana's house.

Sidebottoms were also known to be thrifty. In the days when cereal box-tops could be collected and redeemed for toys, she delighted in supplying her grandchildren with Christmas gifts she had obtained for free. One year five of us received stuffed Tony the Tiger dolls. Poor Grampie must have eaten a lot of Frosted Flakes to earn so many. Nana also supplied us with homemade sweaters, mittens and whatever else her knitting needles created. I still have one of her home-made sweater vests. It has a Fair-Isle type pattern, and it took me more than a decade to grant it the appreciation it deserved. I also have a wonderfully warm afghan (or "af-a-gan", as Nana would say) that she made me for college. It's multi-colored and made with broomstick size needles. She proudly boasted that she was able to use up almost all of her leftover yarn scraps in its creation. It resembled Dolly Parton's Coat of Many Colors. These home-made gifts embarrassed me as a child, but I wouldn't part with them now. I still use that afgan to warm my legs while I'm curled up on the couch.

Just last summer one of my cousins asked me to tell her friend about the time Nana made me a crocheted bikini. This is what happened. At a summer family gathering, Nana wanted to show off her latest creation. It looked pretty cute, and I was encouraged to wear it in the pool. Of course I was willing to oblige. Once I hit the water, however, the yarn stretched completely out of proportion, revealing several of my personal proportions. Fortuitously, a large beach towel quickly appeared and there were no cellphones to capture the incident. I knew that Nana meant well, and it's possible that the directions didn't tell her to line the top with fabric. Also, Nana was almost ninety at the time, and her stitches were probably growing looser. Although her creation didn't work out as planned, at least she picked the right grandchild as her model. Everyone knew I loved attention.

Both Norma and Jack attended Stoughton High School. Norma was a good student, probably capable of being on the college track, but that option never occurred to her or her modest parents. She trained in stenography on the business track and fine-tuned her secretarial skills, In return for her diligent effort, after graduation she secured a good job with a bank. The bank was in the big city, and she commuted by train from downtown Stoughton to Boston every day. She was joined by many of her contemporaries, and I'm sure this was an exciting time of new experiences and independence. My mother was proud of her secretarial skills and I could tell she had felt very sophisticated at the time.

Jack wasn't a huge fan of schoolwork, but he was the fourth of five Sidebottom children to complete all the graduation requirements. His class was two years ahead of Norma's at Stoughton High. They were familiar with each other, but they didn't travel in the same circles. My mom never came right out and said it, but I'm pretty sure my dad was a bit of a hellion. He was very good looking and had a great deal of energy. I will leave the details up to the reader's imagination. After returning from his stint with the Navy, he obtained work as a truck driver for Baker's chocolate company in Boston. He officially met Norma on the commuter train. According to him, she was "the prettiest girl in all of Stoughton." He referred to her in those terms throughout his entire life.

Norma and Jack's partnership was built on complete trust and loyalty. Norma claimed that they married young, naïve and poor - but they "made do with what they had". In the early years of their marriage, circumstances often kept them apart. In addition to serving in World War II, my dad was also shipped off to Korea while Norma joined his sisters in whatever type of supportive endeavor was needed. Jack would have liked to have built a career out of military service like the big brother he idolized. Alfred was ten years his senior, had risen through the ranks and was stationed for a while in Hawaii before settling in California. Somewhere along the line, however, life got in the way. At some point early in their marriage, Jack contracted measles. Sharing my mother's penchant for optimism, my father never mentioned anything about it. I'm not sure how I even obtained that information. It probably came from my Nana or a cousin. Dad would never have considered his illness an appropriate topic for conversation. Just like Norma, Jack didn't discuss hardships or personal issues. It's no secret that soldiers of that era were instructed to keep their war experiences to themselves. It was believed that their families should be protected from such atrocity. This practice carried over to their personal trials as well. And if the armed forces had failed to teach such discipline, they learned it from their parents. My brother and I were inadvertently encouraged to practice the same behavior. *I did the best a drama queen could.*

As time passed and the country recovered, Norma and Jack built up some savings and embarked on a more consistent, suburban life. Jack landed a union job with a supermarket chain. He gradually worked his way up to the position of assistant manager in a local store. They finally found themselves enjoying good health, good friends and good family. The missing element was children of their own. Most of their friends were already raising offspring, so when Norma and Jack finally became parents, mentors and role models were plentiful. I know it has become popular to say, "it takes a village to raise a child," and our village consisted of not only family members, but also many close friends and neighbors. My villagers could always be counted on to buy Girl Scout cookies, school fundraising items and tickets to high school plays. I grew up with what I considered to be a fan base. Probably they were just repaying my parents for offering the same support to their kids, but I valued the encouragement. The village reinforced my ambitious drive and high expectations.

My father's lifelong best friend, Chet Cohenno, was the first person in town to make me a star. Chet had lived most of his life as a bachelor, so he was unable to offer any help in the child development department. What he could offer, though, was free publicity. He was a photographer, and for a short time I was considered quite photogenic. When I was a toddler, Chet used me as a model. Those big blue eyes and chubby cheeks were adorable. I was cute without ever trying. For years a picture of toddler Kathy Sidebottom occupied prime real estate in his studio window. All plans for attaining a modeling career, however, ended right there. The older I got, the less photogenic I became. Subsequent efforts to be cute were met with disaster. The more I tried, the goofier I looked. I was sometimes the kid who didn't purchase the school pictures. Whenever I asked my mother if I was pretty, she would switch the subject to my great sense of humor. Norma and Jack were sticklers for honesty, and Chet managed to avoid me during my most awkward years. Later on, he redeemed his loyalty to my dad by photographing all Drama Club events. No matter what the role, Kathy Sidebottom would be featured in a picture and posted in the local newspaper. As long as I stayed focused on stage business instead of the camera, he would get a good character shot. Never were the pictures glamorous, and sometimes they were downright unattractive - all in the name of good theater. Once Norma actually mused, "it would be nice to see a pretty picture of you in the paper someday." *I'm sure she meant it in a nice way.*

Although their resources were limited, Norma and Jack regarded all aspects of parenting as serious business. When finances allowed, we visited museums, zoos and professional sporting events. In addition to our yearly forays to the farm, we also traveled to as many cultural and historical landmarks as possible. Our parents strove to provide a well-rounded childhood, and they made as many attempts to broaden our horizons as their budget allowed. Our proximity to Boston made a lot of that possible, but sometimes we ventured even farther. Once, my parents saved enough money to take us to the Grand Canyon. We also visited Niagara Falls and Washington, D.C. The year my grandfather died, inheritance money financed a trip to California to visit Uncle Alfred and his family. We even sidetracked our way to Disneyland.

Parents didn't "hover" back then, and John and I were allowed plenty of space to develop our individual personalities and skills. At the same time, we were offered the strong moral guidance needed to make our own decisions. We were taught to budget money carefully, and we learned to live within our means. Both Norma and Jack were raised by productive citizens to become productive citizens, and those values were passed on to us. Raising children, especially during the turbulent 1970s, was a frightening task. My brother and I were as opposite as two children could be, and we both challenged them in different ways. But Jack and Norma remained consistent and firm in their values, even in the face of a rapidly changing cultural climate. Often we were trusted more than we deserved to be, but we never strayed far from the norm. They succeeded in creating a strong, healthy family. We were lucky to have been chosen.

An Extraordinary Segue

I always knew my parents were proud of me. But the Sidebottoms were determined to maintain all stoic Yankee traditions, so thanks and praise were exchanged in moderation. I do recall a certain conversation with my mom regarding my school report card. She explained that since my brother struggled his way through school, they didn't feel comfortable lavishing praise on my academic achievements, especially when it all came so easy to me. I took that to mean that my academic prowess was not overlooked, but shouldn't be flaunted. By today's standards, such an approach might seem strange. But I understood; my self-esteem was not in need of stroking. Yankees are famous for being reserved: public displays of affection and emotion were infrequent, and I was probably more than proud enough of myself. Of all the characteristics I inherited through the Sidebottom's nurturance, humility didn't sink in until later in my life.

I have met only a few adoptees in my lifetime, but I assume we share a desire to express gratitude toward those who raised us. During my freshman year of college, the universe provided my family with an opportunity to publicly glow in pride. I became the Queen of the Sidebottom hometown: Miss Stoughton, 1976! What greater thank you gift could I provide to my family and their friends?

Like most of the events of my life, there is a dramatic story involved with my crowning glory. As we know from our history books, 1976 was America's 200th anniversary year. It was also the 250th anniversary of the town of Stoughton. In celebration of the Sesquicentennial, the Chamber of Commerce decided to hold a Beauty Pageant. I had always loved watching the crowning of Miss America, and of course I dreamed of winning the title one day. But for many reasons, geographical and political included, it was not on my immediate bucket list in 1976. However, just a few months into my first year as a theater major at Boston University, Norma started to get phone calls from the good ladies at the Chamber. They wanted me to enter the pageant.

According to my mother's testimony, she tried to tell the ladies that I wouldn't be interested. I believe her exact words were, "She's not the beauty pageant type." In 1975, I was trying my hardest to establish a bohemian lifestyle with my college dorm-mates in Boston, and she was well aware of my feminist leanings. When she learned how the pageant was judged, and the amount of scholarship money awarded, however, she gave the idea some further thought. Most people don't know about the judging system used in Miss America pageants during the 1970s. As it turned out, 50% of each judge's total score was based on the talent presentation. In addition, another 30% was derived from the judge's interview. It would be difficult for a talentless dummy to win the title. *And I was not one!* Yes, the bathing suit and evening gown portion of the event were judged, but counted as only 20% of the score. The rationale was that modeling a bathing suit displayed a young lady's ability to maintain poise under pressure.

Norma thought I had a chance at that scholarship money.

She called me in my dormitory room and broached the subject. Of course I laughed at her first suggestion. Later on, though, I mentioned it to my roommate, who happened to be the then - undiscovered Geena Davis. She thought it was a great idea. As a matter of fact, I think she dared me to do it. It was only a matter of time before I found myself up to my ears in red, white and blue polyester. The Chamber of Commerce ladies had found 42 girls to compete for the title. They even had to hold an elimination pageant to narrow the playing field. It looked like their kick-off event to the sesquicentennial celebration was a guaranteed success.

With Geena's blessing, I headed home for the preliminary pageant. I made it through the first cut, and there was no turning back. Rehearsals for the show required several trips back to Stoughton from my dorm room in Boston, but fortunately the pageant itself was held during my college Spring Break. Somewhere along the line, my competitiveness kicked in. In principle, I wanted to rebel, but then the quest for the crown started to consume my ambitious nature. My talent presentation involved dressing like a scarecrow and singing "If I Only Had a Brain." *It was, indeed, a no-brainer.* We all wore identical patriotic costumes while performing the opening number, and we modeled matching star spangled bathing suits. The evening gown I purchased for myself was a lacy version of a peasant dress. It wasn't quite formal enough to meet the approval of the

Chamber ladies, but I stood my ground. I don't remember what I wore to my personal interview, but I'm sure it involved polyester and platform shoes.

The pageant itself was not nerve wracking. It took place on my old high school stage, so the setting was familiar. Luckily, the performer in me prevailed. A clarinet-playing friend of mine was the first runner-up, and I won the coveted title. The superintendent of schools placed the crown on my head, and it tried its best to fall off during my victory walk. My mother was accosted by a jealous parent telling her, "This was certainly not a beauty pageant," but sour grapes did not prevent Norma and Jack from being the proudest people in town.

I've heard the expression, "Heavy is the head that wears the crown," but I never thought it would apply to me - and so literally. The plethora of responsibilities associated with being the Queen of Stoughton were far more numerous than I had anticipated. Not only was I expected to move on to the next level of competition (the Miss Massachusetts pageant), but my presence was also required at all sesquicentennial events. Such appearances involved everything from traveling by limousine to the Bicentennial Ball (okay, that was pretty cool) to singing "Pop Goes the Weasel" at a meeting of the Historical Society. (definitely not cool) The Chamber ladies appointed themselves advisors on hair, makeup, clothing and deportment. I even wore some of their clothes. Their mission was to transform a budding hippie into a Barbie doll. Either I was considered inept, or they didn't trust me to style my own hair and makeup, so a local hairdresser was cajoled into donating his services. Every time I an appearance was scheduled, my advisors also scheduled visits to his salon where Mr Andre would style my hair around the crown. In order to avoid conflicts with his regular business, the visit often took place early in the morning before the shop opened. Unfortunately, most of the events were scheduled much later in the day, so I had to wear that crown for hours. Yes, it was heavy.

I earned every penny of that scholarship money. I also learned some bizarre beauty tips. For example, did you know that applying Vaseline to your teeth prevents your lips from sticking to them when you smile? Smoothing baby oil on your legs keeps them from adhering at the thighs. Padding in all shapes and forms is not only allowed, but encouraged in pageants. Bisected Nerf balls make great falsies. None of this came naturally to me, and my life quickly became controlled by pageantry. I acquired false eyelashes, fake nails, and an augmented figure, but in the process I lost my sense of identity and most of my self-esteem. Needless to say, I was conflicted.

The state pageant involved an entire week of rehearsals, celebrations and appearances. Each contestant was housed by a chaperone family and prohibited from communicating with non-pageant affiliated personnel. We could receive cards, telegrams and flowers, but no personal phone calls. For a week I lived in the attic of a home owned by the mother of a former queen. A less persistent young woman might have succumbed to the suffocation of it all, but I had been sucked in, and by this time, I wanted to win.

Although I made it to the group of top ten finalists, I was not crowned Miss Massachusetts. I faced my defeat with chagrin, but my family and their friends did not appear to be disappointed. A large contingent of Stoughtonites had attended the pageant to cheer me on, and my parents were still so very proud. Everyone had been well entertained by the evening's production, and I was happily received back into the fold. I was physically, mentally and emotionally exhausted, but it still wasn't over.

The culminating experience of the Bicentennial celebration took place on the Fourth of July with an enormous parade. Due to the large number of participating units, the usual town parade route was altered. As luck would have it, this year's parade passed right by the Sidebottom house. My parents were thrilled, and they invited all of their family and friends to a cookout before the viewing. I had my own float, and it followed the Budweiser Clydesdales. The design of the Miss Stoughton float was inspired by the little girls' birthday cakes that were popular at the time. The cake's frosting was mounded into the shape of a hooped skirt, and the top of a doll popped up in the middle. They resembled the toilet paper holders my grandmother used to crochet. Members of the Stoughton Little Theater built a huge wooden form for a skirt and covered it with folded tissue paper. I was perched at the top. The former contestants were invited to pull out their costumes from the pageant's opening number (blue hot pants, white boots, star-spangled vests) and sit at my feet. Surprisingly, most of them showed up.

Five miles of smiling and waving is a physical workout. It wasn't long before my jaw and my arms were screaming in pain. The Fourth of July is almost always a hot day, and this year was no exception. The Clydesdales ahead of us were vicious and smelly. Luckily, I was able to hide my lower body under the skirt, so I wore just shorts and sandals. From the waist up, though, the Chamber ladies dressed me in a long-sleeved white jacket and gloves. *And let's not forget that crown.* The parade took hours to move from the starting point to the finish line, and it was very hot and lonely at the top of that fake cake. But when I passed by my parents' house, I summoned up all the enthusiasm I could muster. A large crowd of people were gathered at my house, and I'm sure the loud reception scared the horses in front of me. But at that point I realized the power of the crown. What a great symbol of gratitude to Norma and Jack and a legacy for the Sidebottom family.

And now for the weirdest coincidence of all...

As far as I know, I am the only Miss Stoughton there ever was. I guess that makes me a local celebrity. On the same weekend that I received my banner, my birth father also became a local celebrity, but in a completely different manner. On March 6, 1976, William Bradford Bishop brutally murdered his wife, mother and three sons. It would take me forty-two years to make that discovery. If I live for another forty-two years, I will still marvel at the coincidence and the contrast. In suburban Massachusetts, I represented the pinnacle of wholesomeness. In suburban Maryland, Brad Bishop represented the pinnacle of evil. Thankfully, it took decades to make the connection.

Part Three
Finding Daddy Dearest

It all started by spitting in a tube. Actually, it began before the tube arrived. After a few years of intense theater training at Boston University's School for the Arts, I realized that the life of a starving artist held less glamour than I had anticipated. I was confident in my talent and ability, but my nervous system failed to withstand the constant onslaught of anxiety created by my competitive nature. In other words, I had become too adept at building dramatic tension. I loved performing, but I also craved a stable life: a husband, children, and the wholesomeness I experienced as a child. I relaxed my quest for stardom and exchanged it for teaching certification. *No tension there.* I married young and raised two very dramatic daughters while earning a Master's Degree in Education. Not to worry; drama still remained a major aspect of my life. I became a dance mom and a full time drama teacher. I loved my job and (most) of my students. After all, I faced a captive audience every day. I was never one to pass up a creative opportunity, and the universe tossed many my way. When I found the time, I performed in a variety of productions, and I received more than a few accolades. I admit to feeling a twinge of jealousy when my former college roommate won an Academy Award. *Okay, I'll admit, maybe it was slightly more than a twinge*, but I later became Teacher of the Year, so it sort of balanced out. In any case, I was too busy to spend too much time ruminating.

Since arts education is often considered a frivolous luxury, paranoia runs rampant among theater teachers. Fortunately, I had acquired a Master's degree in Teaching English, so I was prepared to fall back into academia if needed. I managed to hold out as a theater teacher for seventeen years before finding myself involuntarily transferred to the English department. I may not have been the most well-read, but you can bet that I was the most dramatic English teacher in my department. Teaching in general requires an enormous amount of stamina, but the parameters were different in English class. A friend once presented me with a piece of artwork containing the phrase, "Acting normal every day is exhausting." It certainly was.

According to the standards set by test scores, my English language students and I were successful, but the job became increasingly stressful. As standardized testing drove the curriculum, and my competitive nature drove me to excel, anxiety presented itself in the form of insomnia and chronic hives. The agony of the internal conflict experienced during my pageant days returned. Seven years and a million essays later, I became eligible for an early retirement, and I sprinted toward that goal.

Not a moment too soon, the final days of my final year arrived. Exams were held on the last few days of school, so my scholars were engaged in hours of comprehensive standardized testing. As those three long days of testing dragged on, I grew increasingly restless. Usually I embraced the hushed serenity of exam time and used it to plan for the next year. But this time, I had no next year to plan. I'm sure everybody experiences retirement anxiety, and I, of course, had to excel. I wondered what I might do with all my free time. I feared an upcoming addiction to Lifetime Movie Marathons or AARP Casino Bus Trips. To avoid falling into such an abyss, I knew I had better set some retirement goals. A friend had recommended a book entitled, *Inventing the Next Part of Your Life; Women in Second Adolescence.* That sounded like a good start. But before I invented a new part of my life, I thought it might be time to dig into the past. Wouldn't it be fun to take one of those popular DNA tests?

There are several reasons why I had never searched for my birth parents. One reason was based on the old adage, "If it ain't broke, don't fix it." My adoptive family was so supportive and wholesome. Why would I jinx my future? Truthfully, I was worried about what I might discover. The adoption reunion shows on TV seldom mention a dark side, and for good reason. As mentioned earlier, I had already acquired non-identifying information, and the revelations provided logical answers to most of my questions. I knew that I had half-siblings and I was curious about them, but the urge to find them was weaker than the fear of the unknown. My parents and extended family were always open and honest about the adoption of my brother and me, and I wasn't curious enough to expose us all to potential emotional trauma.

Somewhere in the back of my mind, I was convinced that there was an ugly side to my history. Pragmatism had been ingrained through my upbringing, and it seemed like a wise practice.

Once I started googling DNA testing websites, though, I was hooked. I ordered a kit from 23andMe and crossed my fingers. At this stage in my life, I considered myself emotionally stable enough to accept whatever results I might find. My first surprise was the amount of saliva required to fill that skinny little tube.

When I received and registered the results, the online application contained a checkbox for adopted children who were seeking biological relatives. Without trepidation, I checked the box and threw my name out there. Much more quickly than anticipated, profiles of biological family members appeared on my computer screen. Four second to third cousins popped up, and I sent a message to each one. Almost instantly, I was connected to cousin Susan in Portland, Maine. Little did I know that I had hit the DNA jackpot.

My third cousin Susan was not only an instant friend, but also a dedicated genealogist. To say she is an enthusiastic person would be an understatement. She took my spit and ran with it! Almost instantly she knew that we were related on the Tupper side of her family from Maine. It took her no time at all to link me to a host of Mainiacs from the little town of Machias. Coincidentally enough, my adoptive mother's family was from another rural area of the state, and she believed there might even be Leathers crossing through the Tupper gene pool. Susan immediately connected me with other family members, and she was anxious to build my family tree.

Susan and I communicated incessantly. About three months after meeting her online, I decided that we needed to see each other in person. I lived in Georgia at the time, but I was planning a trip to Massachusetts to visit my mom. Susan's home in Portland was less than a two hour drive from Stoughton. We planned an 11:00 meeting at Denny's Restaurant on a Friday morning. My mom was ninety years old when this all started, and she was as excited as me, so she was more than willing to part with my company while I made the trip. I asked my dear friend Kathy from Massachusetts (of the Serendipity tours fame...more about that later.), if she was interested in taking a road trip to Portland, and we planned our escapade. Portland, Maine is a funky coastal town, so we decided to make a girl's trip out of it. We booked a hotel room by the ocean, ate our fill of lobster for dinner and enjoyed the ambiance. The next morning, we took an early walk and visited some local shops. We pigged out on sinful pastries from Holy Donuts, I found a great little book called *Fucking Apostrophes* (every English teacher's lament), and our positive Karma was flowing.

As carefree as we may have seemed, Kathy and I were not totally capricious in our plans. Both of us had viewed our share of CSI episodes, and we had no intention of adding risk to our new lifestyles as retired teachers. Just in case Kathy became hopelessly bored, or Susan turned out to be some kind of psychopath, we devised a code word and an escape plan.

Thankfully, none of this proved necessary, and the three of us immediately hit it off. As a matter of fact, we exuded so much enthusiasm that a family from the next booth couldn't help but notice. "Is this one of those DNA reunion stories?" the mom asked. She was thrilled to hear about it, took our pictures and brought home a great story to share with friends.

As exciting as it was to trace common descendants, Susan was frustrated by her failure to identify my birth parents. According to the background information supplied to the agency by my birth mother, my father was separated from his wife and was the father of two sons. He was described as well-liked and popular. While searching through the Tupper family line, Susan came upon a likely suspect: Clifford Strickland. He had passed away a few years earlier, but Clifford's obituary specifically stated that he was gregarious and well liked. He was also survived by two sons whose ages fell within an age range to be my half-brothers. The accompanying photograph showed a light complexioned man with strong facial features and a twinkle in his eye. It seemed like a perfect match.

The obituary was quite informative, but it mentioned no history of divorce or separation in the family. And even more puzzling, his name was most obviously not Donald, as the Non-Identifiable Information document had been telling me for years. Had my birth mother purposely provided misinformation? Could I have been Clifford's secret love child? If so, how would we find out? And who might be traumatized by the discovery? I began to experience, as I think Poe once said, "gloomy forebodings of ill."

Susan located two of Clifford's surviving sisters. They were 2nd cousins of Susan's and fellow Mainiacs. Susan reached out to one of the sisters, and I can only imagine the conversation that must have ensued. The sisters were shocked, naturally, and they asked for some time to process this information. That's quite understandable. Who expects to hear that her big brother fathered a sixty year-old orphan? Scenes from a high school production of *Arsenic and Old Lace* fluttered through my mind while I waited for the sisters to decide whether or not to bless this endeavor. I had no problem visualizing two elderly ladies seated in antimacassar-covered armchairs sipping tea. I tried to overlook the part in the play about the bodies in the basement.

These women deserve a lot of credit because they kept their minds open, looked at my pictures, read through Susan's information, and embraced the possibility. I wish I had a YouTube video of the conversation and the decision. We were related to a couple of very liberal octogenarians. Even better, they immediately welcomed me to the family and sent pictures of Clifford's two boys at the ages of 11 and 13. Comparing their pictures to school photos of my own from that age showed an amazing resemblance. All we needed now was permission from one of the boys to take a DNA test. William, the eldest, came forward and volunteered. I still admire his integrity. Accepting such a possibility took guts, whether or not his father was alive.

It usually takes six weeks to receive test results. However, eight weeks passed with no data from William's test. Needless to say, our anxiety was growing. So much rested on a little tube of saliva! A phone call to the testing company finally revealed that William's sample had been lost. He was sent a replacement test and we went back to twiddling our thumbs. Thankfully, this time the wait was much shorter. What was revealed? We learned that William, Susan and I are all second and third cousins, so I am not his half-sister. Clifford was not the baby-daddy after all. We had the wrong guy.

I was relieved for the Strickland family. They had been very sweet and generous. I had not been cast in the role of illegitimate love child after all - a role I'm happy to pass up. I'm also happy to say that William and I are now Facebook friends, and all's well that ends well. Although the results were not exactly what we anticipated, it was gratifying to meet some of my Maine blood.

Meanwhile, poor Susan went back to the drawing board and shook a few more leaves on the Tupper family tree. She encouraged me to take a second DNA test, this time through another vendor in order to cast a wider net. Utilizing those results, she found more connections. She was determined to figure the puzzle out, and through some mixture of science, math and voodoo, she eventually did. It wasn't long before she uncovered a breakthrough clue about my birth parent on the Maine/Tupper side of my story. As it turned out, Maine hadn't provided me with a boy after all - it was a girl! My birth mother now had a name - she was Louise! Louise's father, it seems, was Susan's grandfather's first cousin. And then that trail went cold for a while. But the drama was soon to return in unexpected ways.

*Special Note: Susan has tried to explain the procedure to me several times, but my aversion to math and chemistry prevents me from comprehending. For those of you who passed chemistry class, she has provided a thorough explanation of the process as an endnote to this book. I think you will find it fascinating.

I'll never forget the day Susan told me the news. It was one of those long, languid, midsummer days that was begging for diversion. Ironically, I had been working as a CASA volunteer (Court Appointed Special Advocate for foster children) in the rural Georgia town where I now lived and had experienced a rewarding court session. Five sibling boys were about to be adopted by their foster family. As the judge said, "There aren't a huge number of happy ending stories in family court, but this is one." After celebrating with the family, I was headed to meet some friends for lunch. Susan caught me by phone while I was on the way. She asked if I was sitting down. Of course I was. I was driving my car. She then suggested that I call her back when I got home. I knew right away that she had some news. Our mutual respect for dramatic timing meant that neither of us could wait. Getting her to spill the news took little encouragement. And sure enough, it was big news. Susan had found my birth father. After painstakingly constructing family trees for each side, she was able to reverse engineer the data in order to find the answer she was looking for. *Or something like that: the actual process is beyond my realm of comprehension.* This time she was sure she had the right guy. She told me the name and I said, "Wow, he sounds like somebody famous." I wish I had seen her face when she replied, "Oh, he sure is. I'll let you Google him." She provided his name, and the rest is great drama.

Divine intervention provided a perfect parking spot at the restaurant, and I arrived earlier than my lunch dates. That bought me some Google time. William Bradford Bishop did, indeed, sound distinctive. I immediately surmised that he was a Mayflower descendent. After all, the founder of Plymouth Plantation was named William Bradford. No wonder I had enjoyed teaching American Literature for the last several years. I was sure I had inherited the historic genes of a Pilgrim.

Imagine my surprise when my Google search brought me to "Murderpedia." Who knew there was such a thing? The first picture I ever saw of my dad was his mug shot. William Bradford Bishop was featured on the FBI's Most Wanted List. Thanking my adoptive parents for inspiring my wicked sense of humor, I roared with laughter. Given my flair for the dramatic, it made perfect sense that my father was a murderer. Not just any murderer: a major murderer. The star of an episode of *America's Most Wanted* and a *Dateline* exclusive. I looked at the pictures and couldn't help but notice the resemblance. I felt dismay that my adoptive mother had passed away before she had a chance to know. Norma would have loved it! She once joked that I was the secret child of Ethel and Julius Rosenberg. This was even better. The nature of my incredibly wholesome upbringing made his identity even more ironic. I had time to call Susan back. She was relieved that I had responded with humor, as she had suspected I would. We agreed that my news would be the best story at the ladies' lunch table that day. *Once a drama queen, always a drama queen.*

The life and times of William Bradford Bishop is a fascinating tale in and of itself, so I will focus on that later. For now, let's just say that he was brilliant, handsome, and dangerous. I immediately texted the news to my daughters. Kristin's reply chastised me for making inappropriate jokes. She never dreamed I was telling the truth. Her older sister was horrified. Kara had idolized her grandfather Jack, and her one-year-old son was his namesake. She couldn't even begin to imagine what life would have been like with a different grandfather. Needless to say, both daughters were grateful to have grown up with Papa Jack instead of scary Grandpa Brad.

Once my friends arrived at the restaurant, we became those annoying customers who wouldn't put their phones down. Perhaps I should have shown more discretion in my timing; ordering lunch first would have been a better idea. We all agreed that the physical resemblance between Bishop and myself was remarkable, especially around the nose and mouth. His children were three little tow-headed boys with straight blonde hair and blue eyes. They looked more like me than my own children had at that age. We not only shared physical characteristics, but I learned that Bishop had suffered from anxiety and insomnia, as had I, and his mother had once aspired to be an actress. That pretty much clinched it - he was my daddy.

I'm happy to say that finding my birth father didn't really impact my emotional well-being. I have met a few people who were surprised by my candor surrounding the issue. But if they thought I should be embarrassed or ashamed, they didn't know me very well. Perhaps this is a testament to the practice of stoic optimism so prevalent in my upbringing. Or, because the bond established by my adoptive parents was so strong, I couldn't really summon up a sense of emotional attachment to Brad. Maybe my past theatrical training enabled me to detach myself effectively from the situation. For whatever reason, I found the news amusing - another bit of theater in my life. The dramatic timing was perfect.

There is no telling where my imagination might have led me had I made this discovery at a younger age. Would it have altered the trajectory of my life? It might have brought me fame, but was that the type of notoriety I desired? Would I have attempted to exploit the experience to get attention? Surely my emotional reaction would have been more dramatic, but what emotions would I experience? Grief? Remorse? Fear? And what about my adoptive family and support system? How would they have been affected? At this point, I'm choosing to let my adoptive parents' influence guide me. I will not dwell on the past, and I won't waste my time worrying about what might have been. I'm going to just move on toward the future.

So what does a person do when she learns she's the daughter of a murderer? It's not the sort of thing that dreams are made of. And it's too intense for a Facebook posting. This type of news needed to be shared up close and personal - one audience at a time. After my immediate family was informed, members of my adoptive family deserved to know. Norma and Jack had passed away, but I spoke with my brother John. Like any protective big brother, he warned me against "getting involved with that crazy guy." I reminded him of the remote location of my Northeast Georgia home. Since neither UPS nor GPS could locate it, I doubted that William Bradford Bishop would come looking. I also doubted that my birth father even knew of my existence.

Next on my call list was my Aunt Ruth, the oldest living member of the Sidebottom clan. She was fascinated and amused. She agreed that Norma and Jack were having a great time joking about this in Heaven. She even suggested that they might have had something to do with orchestrating the discovery. I talked with several other family members including Karen, a second cousin who had also been adopted. She had recently discovered that her birth mother had Mafia contacts. That's a great story, but we agreed that mine was even better.

In my typical extroverted manner, I embraced a new role as a popular storyteller, sharing my tale with a variety of audiences. Of course I exercised great technique, relating the story slowly and dramatically. *In theater terms, we call that "Milking it."* Not all of my friends knew I had been adopted as a child, so there were many details to digest. I chuckle when I think that I embarked on my own personal coffee and lunch circuit, sometimes meeting with small groups and other times with individuals. No matter how many times I told the story, I never grew tired of witnessing the reactions. The most common verbal response was, "You should write a book!" And that was before I knew the details about my birth mother - but I'm jumping the gun.

I started searching the web for information regarding Daddy Dearest and was shocked by the depth of coverage he and his murderous acts had received. I love a good "whodunnit," but I've never had the time or the inclination to watch many unsolved mystery shows. As another ironic twist, for many years I had been performing with a company that presented Murder Mystery Dinner Theater Shows. I never dreamed that I would be living my own version.

I quickly discovered that Brad Bishop was quite popular within the realm of True Crime mysteries. In the last year, I have met several people who knew all about him. Just another strange coincidental twist happened when my friend Kathy was on a trip last summer to Montana. She found herself sitting next to some young ladies engaged in an audio podcast featuring the story of the Bishop murders. She couldn't resist telling them my story. I can't help thinking of all the years I had yearned for fame. How ironic that my birth father achieved it in one night. That just didn't seem fair. I wonder if he enjoyed being famous ... dead or alive.

The internet is teeming with articles about Brad Bishop and his grisly behavior, and I encourage crime enthusiasts to consult it for details. In the interest of time, I'll provide a brief summary of the incidents leading up to my father's notorious act. According to information gathered from Wikipedia and public news sources, William Bradford Bishop Jr was born to William Bradford Bishop Sr and Lobelia Bishop of Pasadena, California. He was an only child and the product of a middle class suburban upbringing. He came East to study at Yale University and graduated in 1959. After graduation, Brad, as he was called, married his high school sweetheart, Annette Weis, and served in the U.S. Army where he was trained to work in counterintelligence. Eventually he was employed by the U.S. State Department and joined the Foreign Service. He had learned to speak at least five languages including Italian, French, Serbo-Croatian and Spanish, so he was quite useful as an agent. His charisma augmented his communication skills, so he found it easy to navigate his way through the bureaucratic system.

The young Bishop couple spent most of the 1960s living in Europe with postings in Verona, Milan and Florence. They also resided in several parts of Africa, a favorite location of Brad's. During that time, Brad continued honing his academic skills by earning two Master's Degrees - one in International Studies and another in African Studies. Eventually, he and Annette started a family and became parents to three boys. Photos of them show adorable blonds named William Bradford III, Brenton and Geoffrey. Sources say that Brad Bishop loved living abroad, and he was disappointed when they were shipped back to America in the 1970s. Upon his reluctant return to the U.S., they settled in an upscale neighborhood in Baltimore, Maryland. Brad reluctantly accepted his post with the State Department in Washington, D.C. His last official title was Assistant Chief in the

Division of Special Activities and Commercial Treaties. I don't understand what that means, but I love the fact that his office was located in Foggy Bottom. The name implies a great setting for the ensuing mystery.

Neighbors claimed the Bishops were a happy family who enjoyed good health, financial security and social mobility. Brad's father had passed away, and his mother, Lobelia Amaryllis *what a botanical name* was living with them. In 1976, the Bishop boys were the ages of 5, 10 and 14, and they were all enrolled in public school. Annette was taking art classes at the University of Maryland. The family members were heavily involved in school and social activities and seemed to have blended in well with their fellow suburbanites. For Bishop, however, life was far from idyllic. At this time in his life, Brad's struggle with insomnia and depression became overwhelming. Doctor's records documented medical prescriptions for treating these conditions, but there is no way of knowing how well they were working. Mental illness and anxiety are treated as common conditions today, but this type of disorder would have carried a huge stigma among men in the 1970s. Considering the era and the nature of his work, I'm impressed that he sought medical treatment at all. In any case, I'm sure it was a covert operation.

The severity of his mental illness and how it factored into his future actions is anybody's guess. Many, many theories exist, but the most commonly suggested timeline of events reads like this: Brad believed he was in line for a promotion at work, but it didn't materialize. On the afternoon of March 6,

1976, he complained to his secretary that he wasn't feeling well, possibly coming down with the flu. He left work in the afternoon and visited a local hardware store where he purchased a sledge hammer, shovel, pitchfork, and a tank of gasoline. He also withdrew several hundred dollars from his bank account. Later that evening, after the children were in bed, he returned home and bludgeoned his wife, his three boys and his mother. According to Montgomery County detectives, Annette was most likely surrounded by papers and textbooks when she died. The two younger boys were sleeping in their bunk beds, and his teen-aged son had been lying on a mattress on the floor of his room. Lobelia had probably been out walking the family dog when Brad began his rampage, but she became the fifth and final victim when she returned. The dog was not present at the crime scene. The copious amounts of blood found in each respective area led law enforcement to believe that all victims had been taken by surprise - there were no signs of struggle.

After committing the murders, Brad dragged each body to his station wagon and piled them into the back. He then drove approximately 500 miles to a remote section of North Carolina and used his new shovel to dig two holes. In one, he deposited the bodies of his two older sons. The second hole contained the corpses of his youngest son and his wife, followed by Lobelia on the top. She was still wearing the coat she put on when she walked the dog. I wonder if Brad buried them in the same order in which they were bludgeoned. That would be creepily obsessive, but not surprising. He then pulled out his gas tank, poured the contents over each pile of bodies and set both mounds on fire. Murderous mission accomplished, he headed off toward Smoky Mountain National Park, where his deserted car was found days later near a campground in Elkmont, Tennessee.

Strangely, or perhaps arrogantly, Brad took his time moving on to Tennessee. Witnesses claim that he stopped in Jacksonville, North Carolina, to purchase some Converse sneakers on the way, carelessly placing the fee on his credit card. Store clerks who were questioned after the murder testified that he was accompanied by a dog and a dark-skinned woman. The dog belonged to his family, but the identity of the woman remains part of the mystery. Receipts show that he stopped for a meal at the Copper Kettle Restaurant in Wilmington, NC. Witnesses there said he spent time relaxing and bantering with the staff. One witness also noted that he had made racist remarks toward a customer. Of all the witnesses who claimed to have interacted with him during his journey, however, not one described his behavior as suspicious in any way. He has remained elusive ever since.

While Brad calmly implemented his escape plan, evidence of the murders slowly came to light. On the morning after Bishop dug his shallow graves, a diligent forest ranger in Tyrell County, North Carolina, climbed a 120-foot observation tower and noticed a billow of smoke rising above the trees. She radioed another ranger who located and began battling the fire. By the time the ranger arrived at the scene, it was 1:00 in the afternoon, and the blaze had spread to include about three acres of land. Realizing that the fire couldn't be controlled single-handedly, the ranger headed back toward his car to radio for assistance. On the way he spotted a scene that will never be purged from his memory: a pile of dirt and two dead, charred bodies. Nearby was a burning gasoline can, a pitchfork and a shovel. He soon discovered another hole, from which he exhumed the bodies of Annette, Lobelia, and the youngest of the three boys: five year old Geoffrey.

Until March of 1976, the North Carolina county Brad had chosen as a burial spot was a typical quiet, rural area. The discovery of the Bishop bodies instantly changed all that. Funeral hearses arrived to transport the bodies to Chapel Hill for identification. Crime investigators and SBI agents gathered from all over the country, erecting an enormous telecommunications center. Statewide pleas for information were issued, but no one came forward. And of course the area was flooded with reporters from numerous media outlets.

Searching for anything that might resemble a clue, law enforcement personnel tirelessly poured over the sparse evidence and the scene. Finally, when one of the agents took a closer look at the shovel left at the crime scene, he noticed that a piece of the price tag was still adhered to the handle. Although the remnant was miniscule, it contained just enough markings to link its purchase to Maryland. Inventory records traced it to the hardware store visited by Brad Bishop. Finally, a concrete clue had been found and the store manager was immediately contacted.

At this point in the story, it's important to keep the time frame in mind. The year was 1976. The world of rapid fire computer technology had not yet evolved. As a result, the store manager was unable to provide much information. Shovels were common items sold quite frequently in this hardware store. The stock number matched the store's inventory, but there was no way of tracing the purchaser. Since Bishop had withdrawn cash from the bank that day, I assume he hadn't used his credit card, eliminating the creation of a paper trail. What a disappointment. The investigators found no more clues, but at least they were getting closer to the original scene.

Meanwhile, in Baltimore, several days of school and social events passed before the neighbors noticed the family's absence. I realize that the emergence of social media was decades in the future, but I still find it odd that nobody noticed. What a sad commentary on American lifestyles! In retrospect, conscientious acquaintances expressed shame that the family's absence had not been detected earlier. Such circumstances contradict the stereotypical image of the friendly ambiance of life in the suburbs. But I've learned that when dealing with Brad Bishop, contradictions are consistent.

As newspapers began to pile up in the Bishop's driveway, neighbors finally reported suspicious inactivity at the residence. When the local police arrived to investigate, the officers uncovered the most gruesome crime scene any of them had ever encountered. The blood of five bodies was splattered throughout the house. The metallic odor of dried blood permeated the rooms. The ceilings and walls were riddled with dents left from the force of repeated hammer swings. Most uncanny must have been the eerie stillness of an empty house devoid of the victims. The dramatic nature of Bishop's mental state was clearly revealed through the violence inherent in his heinous attacks.

Suddenly, everything came together except a motive and a murderer. North Carolina law enforcement used pictures of the family's corpses to confirm the connection to the Maryland murder site. At the same time, Bishop's bloodstained station wagon was found in the Tennessee woods. In the front seat was a labeled prescription bottle of Brad's antidepressants. I can't help but wonder if he purposely left it behind. Was it a deliberate attempt to throw investigators off track? Bishop was a stickler for details and had concocted a complicated scheme. Sudden carelessness doesn't seem to fit his profile. Maybe he placed the pill bottle in his car as a token of congratulations to the lucky investigator who uncovered it. In any case, this discovery led to a thorough search of the Tennessee site, where no further clues were uncovered. It also expanded the scope of his crime as detectives from three separate states became involved.

In his past, Brad was known as an experienced hiker and outdoorsman, and some still theorize that he donned his Converse sneakers and jumped onto the Appalachian Trail. That would be an easy way to become invisible. Some people think he is still there, perhaps living off the grid as a recluse. Others suggest that he fled the United States, changed his appearance and created a new life for himself. His familiarity with foreign cultures would enable him to move freely throughout Europe or Africa, and he's skillful enough to make himself unrecognizable. All of these suggestions are plausible and easy to imagine.

For more than forty years, various sightings and interactions have been claimed. Former international colleagues swear to have seen him in Europe, and others say he has been spotted locally, but none of these sightings could be confirmed. His name was added to the FBI Most Wanted List, only recently removed due to his advanced age. Theories regarding motive are conflicting, and Brad destroyed the few people who knew him well. The search for Brad Bishop still fascinates and frustrates generations of investigators, both professional and amateur. On a personal note, I wonder if I am his only illegitimate offspring.

Drama, drama, drama! I knew it was in my genes. Although my father's method was unethical to say the least, he attained notoriety. *Not the way I would have done it, but still...* I have viewed coverage of the case on such tv shows as *Unsolved Mysteries, Vanished, Crime Watch Daily, America's Most Wanted, and "The Hunt" with John Walsh.* Bishop's grisly crime has been the subject of newspaper articles and magazine stories, including *Time.* Daddy even has his own song. "The Ballad of Brad Bishop" was written by Steve Lasko and Steve Deady of Charlottesville, Virginia and recorded by the group Coup de Grasse for Adelphi Records. It was released on February 11, 2007, and enjoyed some popularity in the Washington, DC, area. The murders inspired a television movie, several novels, and the book you are reading right now.

Speaking of drama, I wondered just how much my father and I might have in common. Because I lean heavily toward the latter in the Nature vs Nurture character development argument, I'm not really worried about inheriting homicidal tendencies. There are no criminals in the Sidebottom family, and I intend to keep it that way. But after carefully examining Bishop's past, I'm convinced that several of my personality and character traits have been transferred through DNA. Before addressing that issue, though, it would be helpful to know a little more of my birth father's backstory, especially since it contrasts greatly with the background of my adoptive parents. I'll attempt to fill in some of the details between the facts mentioned before.

As we know, Brad was raised as an only child in Pasadena, California. I have seen photographs and home movie footage of a tall, handsome high school football player posing with his future bride, a cheerleader. They could be models for the image of a stereotypical All-American teenage couple. Brad's dad was a geologist and his mom had been an aspiring singer/actress turned housewife. All signs point to financial prosperity, but not wealth. Photographs and home movies illustrate a pleasant, carefree childhood, and I'm sure he enjoyed popularity and self-confidence.

It looks like Brad was a pretty well-rounded young man. Not only was he encouraged to participate in sports, but there's evidence showing that he was also exposed to the arts. His longtime girlfriend and future wife was a talented artist, and his parents held performing arts in high regard: specifically, ballet.

They supported at least one aspiring male dancer, (or danseur, the proper name) even welcoming him to live in their home until he earned enough money to support himself. The dancer later became quite famous, and he plays an interesting role in Brad's story. But we'll get to that later.

Brad was seemingly programmed for success when he came East to attend Yale University. Acceptance to an Ivy League school is a meritorious accomplishment, so I assume that Brad was a poised communicator who presented himself as exceptionally bright and ambitious. Former acquaintances noted that he was an average student at Yale, played a little bit of football, but didn't leave a noticeable mark. Several of his former professors, however, say that he was, indeed, quite bright. He dropped out of Yale for a year to return home and make some badly-needed money, but returned to graduate with a degree in history. After graduation, he married Annette Weis, his high school sweetheart, and that's when he joined the Army and was trained in counterintelligence. This is also where he learned to speak four foreign languages. As he served tenure in several European locations, he seemed to relish the variety of experiences offered by his job. He took full advantage of opportunities to travel and try new things.

At least one of his military assignments required intercepting and communicating with Yugoslavian operatives during the early sixties. Obviously he was a man who was trusted with foreign intelligence and secrets. After an honorable discharge from the Army, he joined the U.S. State Department and assumed

Foreign Service postings in Europe and Africa. He and Annette flourished within the lifestyle of international diplomacy, and that's when their family grew to include three sons. It was while he was living in Florence that Bishop earned a Master's Degree in International Studies from an extension campus of Middlebury University. The Master's Degree in African Studies was earned from UCLA. I'm not sure exactly how that timeline worked, but he obviously was one smart guy. Juggling family, work and school requires stellar focus and energy. It appears that he was self-motivated and driven to satisfy intellectual curiosity as well as social ambitions.

As all good things must come to an end, so did the exhilarating international lifestyle of the Bishop family. As one might easily assume, the field of international diplomacy was extremely competitive. It was commonly known that once the promotions ended, career advancement came to a dead stop, and employees were assigned postings back in the United States. A desk job assignment back home was a death knell. Seemingly without warning, this soon became Brad Bishop's new reality. Since he had experienced such overt success in his past, I'm willing to doubt that he possessed the coping skills needed to overcome his disappointment and sense of failure. At this mid-point in his life, he had no choice but to settle the family into suburbia and adapt to a less stimulating lifestyle. In addition, it appears that the Bishop's European spending habits had been extravagant. It is likely that the family was not financially prepared for a sudden relocation.

Brad and Annette bought a split level home on 8103 Lilly Stone Drive, in an upscale neighborhood called Carderock Springs in Baltimore. Records indicate that the down payment was supplied by Brad's widowed mother, Lobelia, and she came to live with them when they moved in. Brad commuted daily to his office in Washington, DC. His job as Assistant Chief in the Division of Special Activities and Commercial Treaties sounds like a very boring occupation when compared with the flair of his earlier assignments. It is at this point in Brad's history that he began seeking treatment from anxiety, depression and insomnia. Here I suggest that both he and his biological daughter shared similar responses to internal conflict. Both of us struggled through our 40s.

As his family was blissfully swept up in school, sports and community activities, Brad began to disassociate himself from suburban life. His mother, Lobelia, was described as the consummate loving grandma who gladly shared housework and child care responsibilities with Annette. Annette took advantage of Lobelia's assistance and enrolled in graduate art classes. As his family settled in, Brad grew increasingly unsettled. Medical documents show that he was seeing a psychiatrist and held a prescription for Serax, an antidepressant. Also reported was a trial of hypnosis and acupuncture before committing to medication. This sequence of events suggests either a liberal view towards the social sciences or desperation. Perhaps both. How much Annette or Lobelia knew about his suffering is unknown. Brad was good at covering things up.

The clandestine nature of Brad's past work could easily foster habits of secretive behavior. He was a master at managing and manipulating information. According to past acquaintances, Brad was known to keep his personal thoughts and behaviors to himself. Co-workers did not describe him as particularly gregarious, and no neighbor claimed to be his friend. As a matter of fact, nobody seemed to know him well at all. In addition, there were rumors that he and Annette routinely experienced financial difficulties. Most likely the couple found living expenses to be much higher in the United States, and supporting three children in an affluent suburb can quickly create monetary hardship.

Brad's infidelity was also the subject of rumors, claiming that he was occasionally unfaithful to his wife. Since I was conceived during his long-term relationship with Annette, I find that rumor easy to believe. There is no definitive proof, but the accusation fits his profile. I can broadly describe Brad Bishop as a brilliant, attractive man accustomed to a stimulating life. This final phase of his pre-fugitive existence must have felt claustrophobic. I certainly don't question the depth of his psychological disturbance and the sense of desperation that ensued. The unsolved mystery is his motivation to choose murder as an antidote.

Over the years, a few cryptic clues regarding Bishop's motivation have been uncovered. One of the most revealing is his personal journal. It was discovered in a North Carolina flea market several years after the murders. In it, Bishop often quotes passages from Walt Whitman's famous poem "Song of the Open Road," adding his own thoughts as annotations. His connection to Walt Whitman's, and poetry in general, reveals key details about Bishop's state of mind. As a solitary force in American poetry, Walt Whitman stressed the importance of individuality. He was part of the Transcendentalist movement in American literature: a group of writers famous for rejecting society's trappings in search of a simple life. Whitman and other followers encouraged introspection and discouraged unnatural distractions. "The Song of the Open Road" promotes life as a journey toward self-revelation. To Bishop, it inspired an escape from his suffering.

A few of Brad's notes offer insight regarding his mental state. In a journal entry from May of 1967 Bishop writes, "You've got to protect your vision before you. You must make sacrifices, time and effort." Brad is defining a man of drive and determination, (obviously himself) but I wonder about the content of his vision. The average person would hope the "vision before him" would be that of a successful, happy family man. But considering it from a darker side, I wonder if Brad's vision encompassed the contrary? He wrote that passage nine years before he committed his gruesome crime. For how long did his desperation simmer?

Other handwritten notes in the journal mention his purchase of a motorcycle because he "wanted to be alone." His family car was a station wagon: a symbol of middle-class American prosperity. Was he verbalizing a desire for change? Perhaps shedding himself of his family obligations? While living in Maryland, Bishop did indeed purchase a motorcycle and often used it to commute to his job. Not only does driving a motorcycle respond instantly to a need for independence, power and control, it's also useful in executing a quick exit. I wonder how many commutes were spent pondering his escape.

As the pages of the journal turned, Brad's entries and hand-writing became increasingly disjointed. Toward the end of the journal he wrote, "The cursed insomnia makes me sleepy. I cannot reconcile the total absolute indifference of God to me." Bishop's desperation was mounting, obviously supporting the evidence of depression. If he felt that God was indifferent toward him, how might that affect his moral compass? Was he looking for a way to rationalize his murderous plans? Growing increasingly conflicted, Brad wrote, "Love is compatible with ambition, egoism, premonitions of special destiny." At this point I question his definition of love. Is he referring to romantic love or self-love? More than one of Brad's colleagues described him as narcissistic and self-centered. Did these qualities make him capable of justifying homicide? Tortured by the combination of insomnia, disappointment and an overactive imagination, how skewed was his perspective? The answer is not an excuse - just a possible explanation..

Are there similarities between Brad Bishop and myself? Absolutely. There are not only similarities , but also strange coincidences. Physically, we resemble one another. When I look at the pictures of his face, I notice that we share a small mouth, sparse eyebrows, and a distinctive chin. We have the same smile, never very broad when we are posing for pictures. We both appear to be more comfortable in candid shots. Weirdly, I have a mole on the right side of my face that matches a mole on the left side of his. Like the pictures of his boys, I have very straight blonde hair and a round face. I seem to especially resemble the pictures of my biological grandmother, Lobelia. When she was young, she aspired to be an actress and singer, as did I. We both chased and were followed by drama. The hairs on my arms rose when I read about Lobelia's appreciation for dance and her support of a young ballet dancer. Both of my daughters share a passion for dance. My oldest daughter is employed as a dance teacher and choreographer, and my youngest was a professionally trained ballerina. That's just one of many intriguing little details that connect us.

It's also clear that my birth father possessed powerful performance skills. Some might say he suffered from schizophrenia, but I would suggest instead that dramatic talent enabled him to assume several different characterizations. Based on the autobiographical information I've read, I surmised that young Brad was a standout in his hometown, but he was a big fish in the little pond of Pasadena. Although his father earned enough money as an independent geologist to support a Southern Californian lifestyle, Brad was not provided with a trust fund or a prep school education. Blending in with the elite, moneyed crowd at Yale University required some improvisational skills. (I experienced a similar situation as a scholarship student at Boston University) His former college roommates provided descriptions of the varied personas Brad liked to assume and the intensity of his performances. One example involved a sudden affinity for playing squash. Although Brad had no prior experience with any sport more sophisticated than football, he insisted that he was a better player than his cosmopolitan roommate - and he wouldn't let it go. He obsessively set out to not only learn the game, but also prove himself an expert. Eventually Brad succeeded in defeating his roommate, thus taking control of the situation and satisfying his ego. Who knows how much time he wasted in this ridiculous pursuit? He was tenacious, to say the least. Obviously this pattern of behavior would follow him into his future

It bothers me to say this, but it's clear that I inherited Brad's inability to accept defeat and his dogged determination to succeed. A level above stubbornness, it's a byproduct of that competitive gene he passed on to me. I'll admit that sometimes my need for ego-satisfaction overrules rational behavior. Sometimes this involves orchestrating a complicated set of maneuvers. An example occurred during a high school science fair. All of the Honors Biology students were required to enter. Since everything associated with the fair took place outside of class, this seemed to be an unfair assignment. I resented the imposition on my time. At the last minute, in order to save face and maintain my academic reputation, I constructed a totally contrived, yet believable presentation on the Effects of Noise Pollution on Plants. It cost me a few dollars to buy healthy flowers as well as dead ones, and it took some time to fake my data, but I arrived at school with the plants, a tape recording of heavy metal music, and a persuasive poster. I succeeded in maintaining control of the situation, thus satisfying my ego. Like father, like daughter.

Actions like these could be called devious or sneaky, but I considered it creative problem solving. Fortunately, I was provided the opportunity to learn the consequences of my irrational decisions. Much to my chagrin, my science fair escapade did not end when the projects were dismantled. I was awarded a special honorable mention in the category of environmental awareness. With it came the invitation to bring my project to another fair sponsored by a local college. The universe provided a quick lesson in assuming responsibility for my actions. Not only was I required to conduct further research to validate my findings, but I was also forced to face the conscience my adoptive parents had instilled within me. Thankfully, they mixed that with a clear sense of ethics. Would my birth father have provided me with the same moral compass? I doubt it. It seems that Brad Bishop was often guided more strongly by self-interest than morality.

Although there's no evidence that he ever appeared on a stage, Brad was a talented actor. Among his college peers, for example, he was sometimes referred to as moody. Sometimes he cashed in on his natural depression to assume the posture of a sensitive intellectual. When assuming that role, he was particularly drawn to dark class discussions on existentialism. On the other hand, he was also referred to as a charming campus chameleon capable of morphing himself into whatever personality suited the occasion. There's no doubt that he possessed poise and charisma - and a flair for drama. After college, his work with the foreign service required flexibility and quick-thinking - more improvisational skills. He was good at manipulating people in order to obtain necessary information. His life in Europe must have seemed a little like play-acting to an only child who had been raised in a sheltered environment. Photographs from his European years show Brad in theatrical, model-like poses, relishing the status of his position. He easily assessed situations and created desired effects. Those are perfect qualifications for a career in theater: either acting or directing.

After the murders occurred, local investigators questioned neighbors, and most agreed that the Bishops were typical All-American, happy suburbanites. Here, Brad Bishop was convincing in yet another role. Since he successfully vanished after committing his crime, some investigators claim that Brad is still alive and enjoying his persona as a fugitive. His ability to disappear was uncanny, yet we know he left behind easily identifiable clues, such as the price sticker on the shovel and his prescription bottle of antidepressants. He was also bold enough to pay for his new sneakers in a North Carolina store with a credit card. Was he flaunting his ability to commit the perfect crime? How much arrogant joy was derived through his performance? Was he more desperate for attention than escape? Has he assumed a new identity now?

In addition to our theatrical abilities, my birth father and I share appreciation of language and literature. I have always enjoyed reading and writing, and academic stimulus. During the years that I taught high school English, my favorite class to teach was

American Literature. Ironically, I was especially fond of the Transcendentalists. For years, I strived to motivate students in my Honors American Literature classes to plow their way through the writings of Thoreau, Emerson and their cohorts. I like to think of myself as an independent thinker with a questioning spirit, and I was raised in the Unitarian-Universalist Church, a denomination popular among this band of independents.

By all accounts, my birth father was an avid outdoorsman. Like him, I developed a deep kinship and respect for the Earth and Nature. Perhaps he is still alive and living somewhere in Tennessee. If so, he might have succeeded in following the "Song of the Open Road" up some mountain trail. Eerily, I have spent many weeks vacationing in the Smoky Mountains. Is it possible that our paths have crossed?

Another unfortunate similarity I share with Brad Bishop is a diagnosis of anxiety and depression. I understand that the affliction goes hand in hand with ambition and drive, and with low level medication, mine is manageable. I also suffered from severe insomnia for several years before I retired from teaching. The condition hit both my birth father and myself at about the same age, and we both sought a cure through changes in lifestyle. (One far more dramatic than the other) I'm thankful that the level of stigma attached to mental illness has lessened over the years. Medical testing has proven that chemical imbalance can be genetically based, and it's one more thing that's in my genes. Fortunately, I was able to alleviate my agonizing internal conflict by retiring a little earlier than anticipated, and I live in an era that stresses wellness-physical, mental and emotional. But without access to modern medicine, would I have entered a state similar to Brad's? It's a scary thought.

Like Brad, I am also quite physically and mentally active. I require stimulation and variety in order to be productive. Unlike my birth father, I was not at all athletic as a child, as I'd mentioned earlier. My adoptive parents stressed the importance of fresh air and exercise, but we were not a sporty family. Luckily, I discovered the curative power of exercise as a young woman, and while living and working in the South, I used to claim to be on "Boston time" when my brain and body moved quicker than those of my colleagues. I learned the hard way that not all coworkers enjoy being around a perky morning person, so I acquired restraint. My world was sometimes lonely as I fought boredom and impatience with those situations or people who failed to supply me with stimulus. Comparatively speaking as an adult, I can be downright hyperactive. Everyone benefits if I work off some of my energy. Not only physically, but mentally and emotionally as well. I bet I share that quality with my birth father.

According to a theater instructor, one of my faults as a director was that I created my own chaos. I thrived on unraveling disasters -- often of my own creation. I enjoyed the challenge of problem solving, and prided myself when I made the seemingly impossible seem possible. In retrospect, I see now that this behavior was a way of supplying myself with stimulus, making my life more vivid. When Brad Bishop's life became unbearably mundane, he did the same thing. How long it took him to concoct his scheme can't be determined from the existing clues. It might have been a spontaneous reaction to accumulated stress - he just snapped. Or, the entire scene could have been premeditated as the final cure for internal conflict. Who knows what fantasies he entertained while riding that motorcycle or sitting at his boring desk job in Washington, DC.? When he didn't get the job promotion he anticipated, did his ego make him desperate to save face? At what point does mental illness convert irrational fantasies into rational action? In any case, he created pure chaos, and from all outward appearances, the impossible became possible - he got away.

The discovery of my father's infamy has led me to question the path of my own life. For example, I sometimes wonder how this Yankee drama queen ended up living in North Carolina. The truth is that I would love to have retired on Cape Cod, and my husband would head back to Massachusetts in a heartbeat. But after twenty-seven years of living in Georgia, the cost of living up North seemed exorbitant. One of our daughters lives in the city of Wilmington, NC, a funky university city supporting a thriving arts scene. We thought we were headed in that direction. Instead, we stumbled upon a small town on the coast of North Carolina, and we love being close to the beach. We moved to a neighborhood full of Northern transplants and found our comfort zone. Strangely coincidental, though, is the fact that I now reside about 100 miles from the spot where my family's murdered bodies were found. I plan to visit that location soon. Maybe I will travel there on Brad Bishop's birthday, August 1st. His birthday is on the same day as my adoptive brother, John. This is also strangely coincidental. Does that mean anything? Perhaps it's just another weird twist of irony. Maybe my unexpected foray into the True Crime genre has me overthinking things. Or maybe not.

There is one final coincidental occurrence that begs to be included in this story. Based on my research, it appears that Bishop dropped out of Yale in May of 1957. His reason for taking a leave of absence was that he needed to make some money. Is it merely a coincidence that I was born in June of that year? Did he know that he had fathered an illegitimate child? Had he partaken in a financial transaction of some kind? This theory is based purely on conjecture, but it remains part of the unsolved mystery. Maybe I was just a product of a fraternity party or some one-night stand, and he had no knowledge of my existence. Or maybe not. Although Bishop eventually married his high school sweetheart, he and Annette lived for years on opposite coasts. He was single during his college days. There has been mention of his past womanizing behavior, and let's face it, he was a handsome dude. More than one reference claims he could be very charming, and I know he was charismatic. I haven't located anyone yet who can provide first-hand information about Bishop during that time in his life, but it's as relevant as any theory. Maybe I was a guilty detail residing in his conscience?

One way I hoped to gain more information about Brad's college years was by tracking down a former acquaintance. Specifically, I wanted to locate the ballet dancer who lived with the family during Brad's teen years in California. Google provided me with some background information. The dancer's name was originally Joseph Jacques Ahearn, and he was born in Dedham, Massachusetts, in 1934. Coincidentally, this is another tie to Massachusetts - two towns from Stoughton. After assuming the stage name Jacques D'Amboise, he went on to enjoy a long career as a performer, choreographer and educator. He was married to a former ballerina and the father of four children.

Throughout his entire adult life, Jacques D'Amboise had kept in touch with Lobelia Bishop. Obviously he treasured the kindness she provided during his lean years. As the mother of a ballerina and a dance teacher, I can attest that dance, especially ballet, is the most specialized of all performing arts careers and the least lucrative. D'Amboise was truly blessed to have the support of the Bishops. Naturally, I'm curious about the years he spent living with Brad. Their ages would not have been more than a few years apart. It's difficult to know who inspired whom, but obviously both he and Brad shared persistence and determination. Maybe they both were inspired by Lobelia - she probably carried the gene for driving ambition.

I also learned that Jacques D'Amboise was quite a well-respected artist. He is a Kennedy Medal of Honor recipient, featured in numerous movies and ballets as both choreographer and featured dancer. D'Amboise's Wikipedia entry mentioned that he had established a foundation for underprivileged youth in New York City, and at the age of eighty-four, he was still serving as president. Suddenly, I had a lead in establishing contact. I began to research The National Dance Foundation, and uncovered a phone number. First, I called the foundation and left a message saying I wanted to speak with Mr. D'Amboise in reference to Brad Bishop. I never received a response. I tried searching for an email or even a snail mail address for the foundation, but I still came up empty. Finally, I came across a donor page with an email address for the director of fund-raising. Although that address did not connect directly to Mr D'Amboise, at least I had another lead. I sent an email to his fundraising coordinator asking her to please forward an important personal message to him. It took a few months, but I eventually found a response in my snail mailbox.

Mr D'Amboise responded in a most theatrical manner. First of all, he shipped me a copy of his published autobiography entitled *I Was a Dancer*. Chapter Five is entitled "My Brush with Death," which contains the story of what could have happened. As he explains, in March of 1976, D'Amboise was contracted to dance at the Kennedy Center in Washington, D.C. He and his wife had planned to spend the weekend at the Bishop's home in Maryland, taking advantage of a good chance to visit and catch up with Lobelia, Brad and his family. This was the weekend of the murders. Fortuitously, D'Amboise then injured his foot and was unable to dance. Consequently, the performance and weekend trip was canceled. To this day, D'Amboise is traumatized by this close call. Would he and his wife have been included in the massacre? Or would his presence have prevented the murders? And most mysterious of all - why did it all happen? I had contacted Mr D'Amboise in hopes of discovering more details about my birth father's youth. I wondered specifically what he knew about Brad's college days. Instead, I discovered a fairly taciturn man very deeply affected by Brad's actions.

Included in the package that D'Amboise sent was a page of poetry. I assume that it is original, and I wonder if he and Brad had once shared a passion for writing. Maybe D'Amboise had kept a journal when he lived with the Bishop family, and that practice inspired Brad? Maybe D'Amboise introduced Brad to Walt Whitman and "The Song of the Open Road"? Of the six poems he included, two short ones stand out. One is called
"Loss," and it merely states:

'When loss comes, with its dark clouds,
I always think,
"Celebrate and be thankful for *the having,*
You cannot lose what you did not *have.* "

The other poem is just two lines long and is called "It's Good":

"Suggestions for living a life,
Be good, do good."

Although these poems are generic, I can't help but think that they were inspired by the events that occurred that weekend in the Bishop household. It would explain why he chose to send them to me. He also included some handwritten notes recorded on letterhead from his foundation, The National Dance Institute. On September 25, 2018, he refers to his book,

"Dear Kathy...There is much in this memoir that touches on The Bishops... Blood... Lobelia...Annette...
Unexplainable?...MADNESS! BRAIN TUMOR! PARANOIA! MYSTERY! SATAN! LUCIFER!

Above all, TRAGEDY! Let us spend as much time as possible with the GOOD and doing Good.
May you have much JOY in your life...Bye for now, Jacques D'Amboise."

I interpret the text to mean that D'Amboise is not interested in discussing the past. He never answered my questions, but there is no doubt in my mind that he was greatly impacted by the events. The narrative in his book alludes to Brad's possible ties with the CIA, and that corresponds to theories supported by some investigators. I have watched video footage of interviews with D'Amboise, but I have not spoken with him personally. He doesn't seem willing or able to share any leads or clues of explanation.

The next contact I made was with the Montgomery County Sheriff's Department in Maryland. Even though forty years had passed since the murders, the story is still mysterious and frustrating to many. I wanted to contact Detective Popkin who had been the young detective in charge of the original case. I knew from watching video footage that he was still in the area, and I hoped that he was still determined to find a solution. I hesitated for a while before contacting him because I couldn't figure out how to do that with credibility. If I called on the phone claiming to be Brad Bishop's daughter, I might be dismissed as a crazy person. What if I had to leave a recorded message on an answering machine? When I'm nervous, I talk too much: how would I avoid sounding like a babbling idiot? I decided to send a personal letter by way of snail mail. I hoped that a hand-addressed envelope with Attn: Brad Bishop Case would capture his attention. I donned my English teacher hat and crafted the most succinct explanation I could.

After several months, I received a phone call from Maryland. To be honest, I ignored the first message because I thought it was a telemarketer. Mr Popkin did not return my call, but Detective Nelson Rosales from the Sheriff's Department did. We chatted for a few minutes as I filled him in on details, and he asked several questions that validated my story. I explained that I wanted to know if it was possible to compare my DNA with some from the original crime scene. I knew that several suspects' DNA had been compared in the past, so it seemed like a logical request. Detective Rosales asked me to send copies of several documents, including my birth certificate, the results of my DNA tests, and information about my adoptive parents. The request for a copy of my birth certificate stumped me; I wonder if he thought the Sidebottoms were somehow tied to the Bishops? Stranger things could happen, I guess, but the thought of any connection between them and Brad Bishop made me laugh. I also sent pictures because the resemblance is so remarkable. In addition, I provided him with my cousin Susan's phone number as the expert on genetics. Detective Rosales contacted her and she supplied them with all the DNA specifics that proved my ancestry. I understand that the Bishop murder is not a priority case today, and there is much daily work to handle in Montgomery County, Maryland, but I wish that I would hear from them again. I'd like to see concrete proof of my relationship with Brad Bishop, so I will continue to pursue that avenue.

In addition to the detective in Montgomery County, Susan and I have both contacted the FBI. I left the information on their online platform. Susan, however, was interviewed and asked for much more scientific DNA information (not my department! Math and Science are not my friends). They told her that the interview would be audio-taped and archived. I also recently contacted the NPR Radio Show "This American Life." I've heard several broadcasts about some ordinary people with extraordinary stories. I suggested that they contact me about mine. Time will tell whether or not they will bite. But in the meantime I connected with an NBC news producer who worked on an extensive Brad Bishop story two years ago. We've talked a few times, and he seemed to be fascinated by this new twist. He also spoke with Susan about her role in the process of tracing ancestry. Strangely enough, his mother-in-law recently moved to the same area of North Carolina where I live. Since he worked with the Montgomery County Sheriff's Department, I'm hoping he might be able to entice them to get a DNA comparison done.

As for now, I'm still processing the facts. I've tried to be cautious and conscientious about this information. Sharing the story with friends and family is entertaining. Once, I told a friend that I had found my birth father and promised to explain during a lunchtime visit. When we met, she said, "So help me, Kathy, if you tell me Donald Trump is your father, I won't ever believe you again". That's hilarious, but I think the truth is even stranger than that. People often suggest that I call talk shows. The truth is, the whole situation is complicated, and it takes time to explain. As unlikely as the possibility seems, I don't want to run the risk of meeting up with my dangerous father, and I don't feel any type of strong emotional attachment to him. I don't think I need to flaunt my presence. It's a fascinating element of my life story, but I'm not defined by it. My familial loyalty stands firmly with my adoptive family: Jack is my Dad, Norma is my Mom and John is my brother. Those bonds will never be broken; it's as simple as that. Their values are firmly ingrained in my character.

Also, I'm a strong advocate for adoption. I've worked with children and adults within the foster care system as a volunteer CASA, and I've raised two of my own children. I know that families are created in many ways, and the bond occurs over time and shared experiences. A human being is the sum of so many variable factors, and genes are just some of them.

Still, I can't help but wonder what force led me to make this discovery now? Am I being called to provide a voice of warning? Maybe that's true. It has become trendy to jump on the DNA testing bandwagon these days, and I want to advise seekers to be careful what they are looking for. There are so many human emotions wrapped up in identity, and

I've heard lots of stories about disturbing discoveries. I hope that people weigh the pros and cons wisely before taking the risk of obtaining life-altering information. Not everyone is as prone to secrecy as Brad Bishop. Most of us are social animals, and what happens to us affects others. All of these factors should be carefully considered before ordering a test. The field of genetics is made up of puzzle pieces, but it is not a game.

Part Four
Wait! There's More

I thought the drama in my life had reached its climax. I knew who my mother was and I'd just discovered my biological father was a fugitive from justice. What more could possibly happen? The answer is … quite a bit. I was on my way home from church one Sunday, and Cousin Susan called me in my car again. *Thank goodness for hand-held devices.* This time she said, "You have a sister!!" This wasn't exactly earth-shattering news. I knew that two half sisters were out there somewhere. Like most adoptees, I'd grown up looking over my shoulder for long-lost family members. And on top of that, I have a common, generic Anglo-Saxon looking face. People often stop and ask if I am related to someone they know. Depending on the degree of theatrics present in my mood that day, they got either the short response, "People always tell me that," or the long story of my past. If I was having a diva day, the inquirer learned never to ask such a question again.

It turned out that the sister Susan uncovered on my Ancestry match list was neither of the sisters mentioned in my adoption information. This was a third sister - to be more specific, she was a half-sister named Cori, six years younger than me. Cori had recently taken a DNA test, and that's how she popped up on my Ancestry.com list of family connections. The match was identified as a close connection: cousin or half-sister. Because of the emotional and sometimes shocking nature of DNA revelations, I'm glad that Ancestry lists these matches with some ambiguity. Back when Susan first constructed my family tree, it became obvious that both birth parents had no siblings; they were the only children of each set of my grandparents. Therefore, Cori could not have been a first cousin. She had to be a half-sister. The drama queen in me wanted to reach out immediately, but instinct warned me to tread carefully. Somehow I knew such a revelation might shock her, and I didn't want to scare her away. There were so many questions waiting for answers. Instead of answers, however, this discovery unlocked another multitude of mysteries.

My instinct served me well. I contacted her, but I did not immediately suggest that we were sisters. I sent her a message through the website indicating only that we were closely related. I told her the date and location of my birth, and I informed her that I had been born in 1957 and adopted in 1958. Susan also sent her an email identifying herself as a cousin. Neither of us received a response for several days. Needless to say, Susan and I were chomping at the bit to hear from her.

In the meantime, I admit, I stalked poor Cori's Facebook page. *Yes, I have a strong sense of ethics, but I'm also human...and curious.* Her privacy settings were not strict, so she supplied me with a plethora of information. *By the way, thanks, Cori!* The most exciting find was a picture of three generations: my birth mother, my grandmother, and a young Cori. I also saw recent pictures of my birth mother with other family members, so I knew she was still alive. And I found pictures of our oldest half-sister Barbie, and a younger half-sister, Jessica. Wow!! I cannot say that we bear any physical resemblance to each other, so it wasn't as much of a shock as viewing the Brad Bishop pictures. But these people were alive and well - and (mercifully) not featured on any wanted posters. Waiting patiently for Cori's response required all the self-restraint I could muster.

Motivated by Facebook-stalking guilt and impatience, I considered sending another message to Cori. Then I learned that in her enthusiastic message, Susan had told Cori that we were half-sisters. Of course Susan felt terrible for blurting everything right out and wrongly assuming that Cori would know she had a sister out there, but it changed my perspective. Now the stakes were even higher. That crazy imagination of mine kicked into overdrive and entertained every possible reason why Cori hadn't responded. The actress in me suffered through my complete repertoire of emotions. Cori held all the cards in this possible relationship, and I feared taking a chance of irritating her by reaching out again. Eventually, I did., and I'm glad. I tried to verbalize my empathy, apologizing profusely for any trauma she might be experiencing. Finally, a response came through. Just as I had suspected, she was in shock. Her initial reaction, understandably, was denial. She had never heard any mention of me from either her mother or her grandmother, so she assumed I must be mistaken. The information I was able to supply about our oldest sister, Barbie, and the time line I created, however, verified the true story. We both understood that science doesn't lie.

The timing of this shock was terrible, and Cori asked for some space to process what she had learned. She worked in a classroom for children with special needs, and this was the week before school started. As a former teacher myself, I know that's one of the most demanding weeks of the year. Handling all the details needed to prepare for a new class full of kids didn't leave much room in her brain for reassessing family relations. She said that she had taken the DNA test in hopes of finding information about her birth-father, *obviously not Mr William Bradford Bishop*, who had died in a plane crash when she was very young. Another sister was the last thing she expected to discover. My intuition had been correct - she was overwhelmed.

Since I had seen pictures of her, I knew that our birth mother Louise was still alive, and she lived close to Cori. I wondered how this news affected Cori's relationship with her mom. How would she even begin to absorb what she had just learned? Who would she confide in? How many other people were affected? Would she or could she approach Louise about the past? And what exactly happened in the past, anyway? My theatrical conscience was consumed with guilt for traumatizing poor Cori and her family. On the other hand, I knew these were my blood relatives and this was my heritage. After discovering my mass-murdering birth father, what could be worse? They seemed to be nice people…dare I say, even "normal"? I wanted to give Cori all the time she needed, but there were so many questions awaiting answers.

At this point, I have to say that viewing pictures of Louise elicited no emotional response. Maybe Brad Bishop had sucked my emotions dry, or perhaps it was due to a detachment skill I had learned in acting school. Either way, my response was pragmatic. As I described at great length earlier in this book, my adoptive parents provided me with a strong sense of family, and I never felt the void that other adoptees talk about. Some have mentioned challenges to their identity, or feelings of inadequacy. I never felt that way. It's also true that my physical characteristics resemble the Bishop side of my gene pool. I wasn't able to see much resemblance among my maternal family members.

Of course I understood and respected Cori's need for processing time. After all, it took me sixty years to emotionally prepare for this journey. I can't imagine how it must feel to stumble onto an unsolicited discovery like this. I couldn't help but think back to my time as a theater student and teacher. Once again, I'd created chaos, however unintentionally. More than once in my life, I've been asked not to drag innocent victims into my own personal melodrama, but oops! I did it again. I tried not to beat myself up about it. At least now I had Lobelia, Brad, and their genes to share the blame.

I don't want the reader to think that I was totally agonized by this experience. My adoptive parents taught me to be a very positive person, after all. By this time, it was August. As the plot of my story continued to unravel, friends grew more dependent upon me for summer doldrum relief. I was in my element and happy to oblige. This serial was becoming more engaging than a midsummer miniseries, and I entertained a variety of appreciative audiences. The saga also supplied Cousin Susan with unparalleled bragging rights among her genealogy group. My dear friend Kathy in Massachusetts said one day, "I'm so glad you're my friend. You keep my life from getting boring."

I still had the best story at the lunch table. I'll never forget a gathering of women from my Unitarian-Universalist Fellowship. As I mentioned at the very beginning of this search, several of us were involved in a book study of the piece *Inventing the Next Chapter of Your Life: Women in Second Adolescence.* Several months had passed since our last meeting, and we were taking turns catching each other up on our progress. Only the hostess of the gathering knew what had transpired in my life, and we both sat smugly listening to everyone else's story. Ironically, all of the sagas being shared that day were a bit bizarre. One woman had lost her beloved goat, and she described the emotional process of finding a new companion for the lonely pet left behind. Another woman talked about her travels to California to participate in a spiritual quest with a woman who believed herself to be the reincarnation of Jesus. This story was followed by a long diatribe narrated by Jane, who shared all the details leading up to her installation of a personal bidet. (*I promise I am not making any of this up.*) Drama Queen Kathy sat patiently, encouraging the buildup of dramatic tension. When I finally spilled my story, it was received with dropped jaws and silence. The shock was finally broken by Jane's cry, "I can't believe you let me go on and on about a damn bidet!" *My feelings exactly.* Her dramatic timing was also impeccable, and it goes without saying that I immensely enjoyed the moment.

Months passed before I heard from Cori again. I tried to keep it focused, but my mind reverted into theatrical mode, once again creating chaotic scenarios. I berated myself for ruining relationships and lives. Finally, a communication break came from Cori's son, Ronno. I have since learned that his name is really Ron. Apparently it was followed so often by the word "No," that the two words ran together and became his childhood nickname. I just loved hearing that endearing story. It seemed like something I might have done. Ronno is a great guy with an outgoing personality, and the nickname suits him. I'm not sure what, if anything, his mom told him about me, but one day his name suddenly popped up on my Ancestry.com family list. Both Susan and I wrote to him right away, and he was the catalyst we needed to break the communication block. Ronno was friendly, gregarious, and fascinated by the whole story. When he was told about my birth father, he jumped on that information like the good millennial he was, soaking up all the information available on the internet. He spoke with Susan several times, sharing tidbits of family history. Eventually he became willing to serve as the go-between and assumed the responsibility of bringing us all together. I learned all this information from Susan. Several months passed before I was included in the communication chain, and that was somewhat by choice. I was intimidated by my own imagination, and I didn't feel confident about initiating conversation. I envisioned myself as not only the "red-headed stepchild" (coincidentally, I actually have a red-headed daughter), but also the Grinch who stole Cori's family stability.

One day in December, Susan called with some good news. We often connect at the strangest times. This time I was sitting down in a chair instead of the seat of my car, but it was on a balcony at a condo in Hawaii. At the time, she was the last person I expected to hear from. Susan let me know that she and Ronno had been talking quite a bit, and that Cori really wanted to get to know me better. Susan reassured me that I hadn't ruined any lives, and I released some of the bad mojo that cluttered up my mind. *That's pretty easy to do in Hawaii.* Cori and I still hadn't connected by phone, but Facebook became a conduit for building common ground. Cori, Ronno, Susan and I all became Facebook friends. Now I could search without guilt. It allowed us to learn about each other and establish some commonalities. With the holidays approaching, we were provided with lots of opportunities to observe families and festivities and establish a frame of reference.

After the first of the year, Susan told me about some plans she had made to stay with some friends in Florida. These friends lived in the same vicinity as Cori, Louise and Ronno. Together we thought about orchestrating a face-to-face meeting. Since I lived only one state away in Georgia, it wouldn't be terribly difficult to get together for a weekend. I felt some instinctive trepidation, but I attributed it to social anxiety and made a flight reservation for a weekend stay in February. By now I had shared several entertaining email exchanges with Ronno, and he sent a few encouraging messages stating how excited he was to have us all be together. Through Ronno and Facebook, I had learned a little bit of family history. Ronno had a sister named Kristen. Coincidentally, I also have a daughter named Kristin. Cori's Kristen has adorable twin daughters who are very close to their grandmother, great-grandmother and Uncle Ronno. Cori had been married to her husband for more than thirty years. They originally lived in Massachusetts, where we were all born, but the family eventually relocated to Florida when the children were small. I learned that Barbie, the oldest sibling, still lived in New England, not too far from another half-sister named Jessica, who is the youngest. That's a good bit of information to garner without ever having met. (And if you're keeping track, that's five offspring for Louise thus far.) I also knew that my birth mother was still alive and living with her husband in Florida. It became clear, however, that she had not been told anything about me. Since she had kept my existence a secret for all these years, I don't think anyone knew how to broach the subject.

Early 2019 was a sickly season. I try to be proactive about maintaining good health, but one rotten cold after another attacked my body. Susan experienced the same dilemma. We joked about sharing germs through phone lines and the internet.

Poor Susan was eventually diagnosed with the flu. Traveling to Florida was out of the question for her, especially since the friend she was planning to visit was battling cancer. I am usually a very outgoing person, but the idea of initiating the family meeting on my own fell way outside of my comfort zone. We eventually canceled the visit, and I'd be lying if I didn't say I was a little bit relieved. Sometimes determination interferes with my intuition, and I probably should have paid more attention to the trepidation I experienced at the start. I think the universe was telling me that this was all happening too fast. I do need to add a plug here for my travel insurance company. I don't always purchase travel insurance, and I'm surprised that this time I did. Since my claim for cancellation did not fall into any of the standard categories, I had to explain the circumstances. I chose the "cancellation of travel companion" option on the claim form even though Susan and I were not planning to travel on the same airline, nor were we even flying on the same day. I wrote a short narrative explaining the purpose of our trip, however, and my claim was accepted. The stars were aligned in my favor.

When all parties were informed of the cancellation, we probably issued a communal sigh of relief. I think we all needed a little more processing time. The concept of this new extended family was still young, abstract and a bit surreal. As long as we hadn't met face to face, the reality didn't yet exist. Cori promised on Facebook Messenger that she would call during the following weekend, and I waited. Friday evening passed. I know most teachers are exhausted on

Fridays, so I didn't expect a call. But when Saturday came, I began actively waiting, trying every trick I knew to distract myself until the phone rang. But it didn't. On Sunday, the suspense worsened, and I made myself as busy as I could. By day's end, all of my closets were cleaned, weeks of lesson plans had been created, and for the first time in my life I watched an entire NFL football game on tv. That's a sure sign that I was frazzled - I've never been a football fan. By Sunday night I was disappointed and downright cranky. As the kids would say, "I had all kinds of feels." In retrospect, I realized that we had never scheduled a specific time for the call, and I nagged at myself to pay greater attention to detail. The logical side of my brain proposed a myriad of practical excuses, but the other side of my brain was in emotional overdrive.

I knew Susan was waiting to hear all about the conversation, and I hated reporting my disappointment. As expected, she commiserated, and we concocted all kinds of scenarios intended to make me feel better. What we found out in a few days added yet more drama to the story. Here's what happened: My birth mother's husband had been scheduled for hip replacement surgery in the near future. Understandably, his balance and strength were not always stable. On Friday night, he took a fall and hit his head. The accident proved to be fatal, and he passed away. That's not even close to any story Susan or I had created. Poor Cori! Just as she was recovering from one incident of shock, she was now faced with grief. Also, she was the sibling who lived closest to Louise, so the lion's share of the ensuing responsibilities fell upon her. What a mess of emotions she must have experienced. The last thing she needed was an awkward phone call with a mysterious half sister. Once again, the inherent theatricality of my life loomed large.

At this point, a diagram or scorecard would be helpful in order to help a reader keep track, but I will attempt to explain my understanding of Louise's family history. Hold on to your hat because this is complicated, and I might not have it quite right. I'm also unsure of a few facts, but I'll do my best to explain. As mentioned before, Louise gave birth to her first child, Barbie, in 1953. Louise married Barbie's father, but it didn't last. After the marriage dissolved, Barbie was raised by her grandparents in Lubec, Maine. How or why Louise ended up giving birth to several children in Massachusetts is a secret, and one she has managed to preserve. We'll call that period of her life the lost decade. At the end of the lost decade, Louise gave birth to Cori. Cori never knew her father and was told that he died in an airplane crash when she was a baby. Cori also has a brother David, but I'm not sure who his birth father is, and I've never felt comfortable about asking. After Cori's father died, Louise finally met the love of her life, Bob. Knowing this brings me a sense of comfort and relief. I was told that Louise eventually reconciled with her father, and he was the person who introduced Louise and Bob. They married, and Bob adopted Barbie, Cori and David. Bob and Louise were blessed with one more child, Jessica. All of the children eventually ended up living together in Massachusetts, and Bob was revered by each of them.

Louise was married to Bob for thirty years, and his death brought shock and sadness to all members of the family. Bob and Louise had retired to Florida and Cori's family had subsequently moved nearby, so they all gathered together there to support Louise and participate in Bob's funeral arrangements. In her characteristic way, Cori orchestrated the details.

Everybody knows that milestone family events require strength and stamina. Throughout this difficult time, poor Cori was also burdened with a huge family secret. Not only had she uncovered shocking information about her mother's past, but she also knew that Ronno was in on it, too. I don't know how much of the secret she had shared with her siblings. Cori had long ago assumed the role of family caretaker. Did this include preserving her mother's secrets? None of the other siblings had taken DNA tests. This was certainly not the time to approach Louise, but was this an appropriate time to be sharing her secret with the rest of the family? I wonder what was worse: keeping the information to herself or dragging her siblings into the chaos. I can't even decipher where her responsibility began or ended. Of one thing I am certain, however. Cori is a strong woman. I don't know the circumstances, but eventually the secrets were revealed. Only one sibling, David, was purposely kept out of the loop for fear that he might confront Louise, thus creating more trauma. Since he lived in Colorado, it was hoped that the distance would help preserve the duplicity.

Meanwhile, Susan and I were waiting patiently for an appropriate opportunity to connect with more of my new extended family. But DNA wasn't done with us yet! This time I beat Susan to the punch, and I was the one to call her. Since she is my cousin, and she has been a tireless detective, I feel as though my story is also her story, and I share my private Ancestry.com page with her. But it was most unusual for me to learn anything before she did. I was positively gloating when I called her and announced that I had found another sibling. Like me, she assumed it was the unknown little sister born and adopted two years after me. But no, this baby had been wrapped in a blue blanket. I'll never forget the conversation. I milked the announcement for all the theatricality I could get. Here's how it went. I said, "Guess what, Susan, I have a brother." She answered with, "Yes, we know you have a brother named David." "Nope," I said, "this is an older brother." She claimed that was impossible. When she looked at my page, however, she was shocked, but she gleefully admitted she was wrong. Susan loves drama almost as much as me.

My older half-brother Marc popped up on Ancestry.com without much of a flourish, but it was a huge surprise for everyone. Like me, he had been placed for adoption in Massachusetts. We communicated right away and shared an instant rapport. His birthplace was listed as Tewksbury, Massachusetts, but he had been adopted through a different agency. He grew up on the North Shore of the Bay State, in Salem. He was born just two years after Barbie, and I was born just two years after him. (And for those of you who are counting, we're now up to six siblings-seven kids in all.) Marc and I shared a lot in common: we both grew up knowing we were adopted and had been blessed with wonderful parents. As my parents had adopted an older brother, his parents adopted a younger sister. His childhood had been as stable as mine.

Both Myles' parents and mine followed a typical route to form their families. Couples who adopted one child from an agency often returned seeking another of the opposite gender. Single parents were rare in those days, and girls who became unwed mothers would often be known to disappear on alleged extended visits to distant relatives. The distant relatives were really group homes affiliated with adoption agencies. The mothers were provided with prenatal care and maternity services until the babies were delivered. Many of those mothers surrendered their newborns to the agencies, providing infertile couples with their opportunity to parent. Adoption fees were affordable, and that system seemed to work. I've always wanted to believe this to be a good system for all involved. There are, of course, horror stories about black market babies and unfortunate women who were left without choices, but I hope I'm correct in my assumption that most agencies during our era were affiliated with compassionate organizations.

Just like me, my half brother Marc had also waited until he was in his sixties to search for birth parents. He was retired, the father of four children, and his first grandchild was on the way. Our scenarios are very similar. Also like me, he knew he had an older sister named Barbie, and they lived fairly close to each other in New England. Marc knew that he and Barbie shared the same birth father, making them full siblings. This detail contradicted my previous understanding of Louise's past, and further complicated matters for the rest of the family. As bizarre as this story was becoming, I have to say I was relieved to find a partner in crime. Suddenly I was not the only unexpected guest at the table. It took a few days to schedule a phone connection, (this time I was far more specific about scheduling a time) but when we did, he and his sweet wife, Sharon, were gracious and informative. I sent him copies of my adoption documents, including the information reported by our birth mother. We shared some pictures, and we remarked about our similarities in coloring and stature. Marc and I also shared the same attitude about our past. We both grew up knowing we had been adopted and were surrounded by stability and support. Both of us felt secure in our identity, and we shared a desire to thank our birth mother for giving us the opportunity to thrive.

Marc had previously obtained non-identifying information from his adoption agency. Although It was not The New England Home for Little Wanderers, the format was similar. According to his notes, Louise had visited Marc frequently while he was living in foster care. We assume that she was trying to avoid placing him for adoption. We can only guess at her circumstances and wonder about what might have been. *More questions!* Our older sister, Barbie, was living in Maine with her grandparents at that time, so how did Louise end up in Massachusetts? And why? Louise couldn't have been more than twenty years old. How did she support herself? Where was the father of her first two children? The birth certificates state that he was a hotel owner who lived in Florida. It was beginning to look like my gene for theatricality was not solely attributed to the Bishop branch of my family tree. Louise's actions exhibited a flair for the dramatic, too. I guess I inherited a double dose.

As part of the adoption process in the 1950's, a new birth certificate was created for each adopted child. Certified by the Commonwealth of Massachusetts, mine clearly stated John and Norma Sidebottom as mother and father. I had often wondered what happened to my original birth certificate, and Marc informed me that those documents had been archived. A 1970s ruling made them available to adoptees in Massachusetts. He had obtained his, and it named the same father as the man listed on his family tree. After he directed me to the website, I filled out the form, sent a $35 check and eventually obtained mine. It was a copy of the official court document from the Bureau of Vital Records, but hand-written across the middle were the words "Conv to Sidebottom." I guess that means "Converted"? The handwritten scrawl provided a quaint informal touch to a very important document.

Holding that official document in my hand impacted me more than I had anticipated. Up until that moment, I think the actress in me felt as if I were playing a role in a great melodrama. It might be a tacky cliché to quote Shakespeare here, but "All the world WAS truly a stage, and the men and women merely players." Now it was real life.

My original birth certificate listed my name as Darlene Marie, Louise as my mother and the same father as Barbie and Marc. What? Science had told me that wasn't true. I wondered if, since the wrong father was listed, was my birth certificate invalid? *Was I an alien after all?* Now I had even more questions. Why did Louise choose to list that name as the father? During her interview at the adoption agency, she provided intricate details about a different man named Donald. What was that all about? Was she uncertain about my father's identity? Was she fantasizing? Was she protecting someone? Who was Donald? And again, I ask "Where the Hell was William Bradford Bishop?" How did she ever hook up with him in the first place? According to his biographical information, he would have been a student at Yale. Connecticut isn't far from Massachusetts, but how and where did he meet Louise? Had she crashed a frat party? *How do I purge scenes from Animal House from my brain right now?* Flash forward to 1976 - Had Louise heard about the Bishop murders? Did she know she had given birth to the child of a murderer? What about that daughter who was brought to the agency two years after my birth? Now referred to by my half-siblings - supporting cast members in this soap opera - as "Jane Doe," we're hoping that she shows up soon on our Ancestry list. Who is her father? What if William Bradford Bishop is her father, too? DNA can answer the final question, but only Louise knows the rest…and she is not talking.

The cast of the drama increased. By the spring of 2019, almost all of Louise's offspring as well as several grandchildren were engaged in this mystery - almost everybody except the main player - Louise. Just to recap: the cast of characters included, in chronological order: Barbie in New Hampshire, Marc in Massachusetts, me in Georgia, Cori in Florida and Jessica in Massachusetts. Brother David in Colorado had not yet been informed. And "Jane Doe," the third child surrendered for adoption, was still missing. I'm guessing that the age span between oldest and youngest is at least fifteen years. Through interactions with Ronno, Susan and I gathered as many puzzle pieces as we could. Still, only Louise could put them together, and she never revealed an inkling of evidence. In the words of Ronno, "We will just have to let Grandma take that with her to her grave."

As I've shared my story with other people, I've noticed that reactions tend to fall into one of two categories. One side says that I have a right to know my history, and they advocate confrontation and transparency. The other side is satisfied with the knowledge I've gained and encourages the preservation of privacy. Once again, I'm experiencing inner conflict, but my instincts are compassionate. So, I am leaning toward the second direction, fully aware that Louise lived in an era entirely different from mine. And she was so young. I can't imagine the emotional trauma she endured as a result of her actions. According to her testimony at the adoption agency, she had been raised as the only child of strict Yankees - a culture known for stoicism and restraint. By the time I rolled around, she was once again, for the third time, a "girl in trouble" and most of her late teens/early twenties had been spent that way. If the portrait she painted of herself is accurate, my instinctive reaction is empathy.

On the other hand, I have no way of knowing how accurate the portrait is. Years of experience raising and teaching teenagers has taught me the difference between reactive exaggeration and realistic response. So, I have more questions...Just how strained was Louise's relationship with her father? When interviewed by the adoption agency, was she speaking from selective memory, looking for a scapegoat, or was she truly scarred by her father's past actions? Psychologists would most likely agree that an insecure relationship with her father would motivate attention-seeking behavior with men. The obvious consequences pointed in that direction. Whatever the cause, I'm not judging her actions. In the end, she made responsible decisions.

As the winter of 2019 turned to Spring, I became bolder and more anxious to connect with Cori. Although I had spoken several times on the phone with Marc and his wife, I had yet to hold a verbal conversation with any of my other family members. Both Susan and Marc had reached out to Barbi and Jessica. They assured me that they hadn't perceived any traces of hard feelings on the part of any new-found family members. My drama queen gene, however, wouldn't let go of my guilt about stirring up this mess. I thought I had given up creating chaos, but I guess that habit crept back when I wasn't looking. At my age, I should know better than to second guess another person's feelings, but that's my automatic default mechanism. I detest confrontation, so I fear unpleasant encounters. (I wonder if this is a quality inherited from Louise - it seems to fit her profile.) I was in need of reassurance, and too sensitive to seek it. I was hoping that somebody else might take the first step and initiate contact. There had been an exchange of phone numbers, and maybe even a text or two, but a personal phone call would make me feel better.

Once again, Ronno came to the rescue. One Saturday morning, I resolved to dial his phone number. I was actually back in my car again, and I knew I had two hours of driving ahead, so it seemed like a good use of time. As it turned out, Ronno was working and unable to talk, but later (when I wasn't driving) we texted and made an appointment to talk later in the evening. At some point during that afternoon, Ronno and his mother came up with a great idea. He would go to his parents' house, and we could all chat together on speaker phone. (What we needed was a Zoom call - but this was pre-Covid) Eventually I enjoyed a very friendly, if not a bit awkward conversation with Ronno and Cori. The topics we discussed were generic - children, grand-children, jobs, and the experience of growing up in Massachusetts but relocating to the South. Our lifestyles were very different, but we shared enough in common to keep the conversation going. Cori worked in a classroom, as had I. She moved South as a result of her husband's job, and she obviously adored her children. That much we had in common. The herd of elephants in the room - Louise, William Bradford Bishop, Marc and the other siblings - were not mentioned. As I said, it was just a friendly, pleasant call. I felt better.

Apparently the universe was not content with just a phone call. It soon arranged a face-to-face meeting. In keeping with this story's theme, it happened in an amazingly coincidental manner. Every June, members of the extended Sidebottom clan gather on Cape Cod. (Lest the reader confuse us with the venerable Kennedy clan, I assure you, our accommodations are far more humble.) I've mentioned the importance of maintaining Sidebottom family traditions, and this summer's get-together was no exception. I had made plans to be there, staying as usual with my brother and his wife for just a few days. As Benjamin Franklin once said, "Fish and visitors both stink after three days," so I keep my trips to the Cape short and sweet. After visiting with my family, I usually move on to other parts of Massachusetts and spend some time with my New England friends before heading back to my home in Georgia.

This summer, I thought I might be able to arrange a visit with my half-brother Marc and his wife Sharon. As luck had it, they happened to be free on the weekend that I suggested, and we decided on a date and time. I was beyond excited. Since Marc and I shared so much in common, I felt no anxiety about this meeting at all. They had previously met with our youngest sister, Jessica and her husband, and I wanted to hear all about it. Marc had commented that the meeting started out awkwardly, but it ended with lots of laughs. I expected the same. Judging from our phone conversations, I was convinced that both Marc and his wife Sharon were very sweet, authentically kind people. For example, I remember once saying , "Between our birth mother's secrets and my father's murderous tendencies, it's a wonder that I have any sense of ethics at all." Susan responded with, "Kathy,

I'm sure that when God chose the genes you would develop, he chose wisely." What a sweet thing to say - and I hope it's true.

Multi-taker that I am. I thought it would be fun to add my friend Kathy to the mix. I have mentioned my dear friend Kathy from Massachusetts before. She had joined me on my Portland escapade to meet Susan, and she knew all the details of my continuing saga. I asked if she might be interested in taking a weekend trip to the North Shore of Massachusetts, and she immediately agreed. I hadn't visited Salem, Rockport or Gloucester in at least forty years, and I knew we would have fun exploring. Since I was unfamiliar with the area, I suggested that Marc pick a restaurant, and I knew my trusty GPS would help us find it. When I mentioned that Kathy would probably tag along, he genially replied, "the more the merrier!", and we had a plan.

Meanwhile, the pace of life in the Gillcrist house was about to become cyclonic. Over the past few years, my husband and I had been planning to officially retire and relocate, but we were waiting for the real estate market to strengthen. All of a sudden, the market resurged, so we activated the plan. Just to further complicate matters, our realtor convinced us that the house needed to be staged. This process involved the relocation of most of our furniture and personal belongings. Yikes! Over the course of a day, our home of fourteen years became a streamlined showplace. The minimalist look was very attractive, but also disconcerting: we never seemed to know where anything was. My home became a metaphor for my brain: it looked calm and peaceful to the outside world, but a million little details had been relocated. Once again I found myself dealing with chaos, but at least I wasn't responsible for its creation this time.

Soon the house was sold, and the next thing I knew we were organizing our move to the coast of North Carolina. Since the retirement plan also involved serious downsizing, an estate sale company was called in to categorize everything, pack up those possessions that were accompanying us, and prepare the rest for sale. The level of chaos doubled exponentially each day.

At this time in my life I felt like I was living in the eye of a hurricane. So many details required my attention that staying focused was a daily challenge. Just to add some fuel to the fire, I was rehearsing with a regional theater company for an upcoming production. It was an American adaptation of a French farce, no less. I needed to memorize a great deal of dialogue, and much was written in double entendre style. For most people, such a task might seem daunting. For a drama queen like myself, however, it provided a mental oasis from the disorder swirling around me: a focal point for my squirrelly brain. And of course, there was drama: my comfort zone.

One evening, on the way to rehearsal, I decided to give Ronno a call. *From my car, of course.* We had texted back and forth once in a while, but I wanted to touch base by phone. I have no idea what caused me to choose the particular time and place, especially since reception in that driving area was often poor. I'm sure a more powerful force was at work. I told

Ronno about my upcoming June trip to Cape Cod and shared my excitement about meeting Marc, Sharon, and possibly Jessica and her husband Frank. He asked me the dates, and when I told him, he responded with a very dramatic "Hmmmmmmmmmm, that's interesting." Now Ronno was being dramatic, and I was not about to let that comment pass without an explanation. He told me that he and his family were planning to travel from Florida to Massachusetts on that same weekend. There was a family wedding in Boston, and they were all invited to attend.

What an opportunity! The Universe had plowed right through my psyche's static, forcing me into clear focus. Four out of seven half-siblings would be in Massachusetts at the same time. Ronno and I agreed that this was too uncanny a coincidence to ignore. I immediately offered to meet at any time and any place - even breakfast at Logan Airport if necessary. Ronno carefully reasoned that he didn't think his parents had even made flight reservations yet, and scheduling was still up in the air. I've been known to jump into things, and I realized that not all people share my impulsiveness, (Another quality I probably inherited from Brad Bishop) but this was an event waiting to happen. Ronno was now responsible for presenting this new proposition to his family. Meanwhile, my mind concocted a million possible scenarios.

Unfortunately, I never heard back from Ronno. If I'd had more spare time, I would have wallowed in my disappointment. But I managed to subvert those difficult feelings. I resigned myself to conclude that my presence would probably cause an inappropriate disruption to a family gathering, and that wouldn't be fair. I didn't want to push myself onto an unwilling audience. I swallowed my pride and persistence, and I pushed the negativity away. My focus returned to the French farce.

In the meantime, our moving date was moved up a few weeks, so the pace of my life became manic. The logical behavior most people exhibit when presented with major life changes is to simplify in order to focus. That would mean canceling future plans or diversions, but I was having none of that. My brother John called to ask if I was still coming to Cape Cod in June. "Of course," I answered. My friend Kathy offered to cancel our reservations on the North Shore. "Why?" I asked. I've never been one to follow the norm, and I've always believed that I should take advantage of all opportunities. Back when I was in high school, I was cast in the title role of the play *Auntie Mame.* Since then, a favorite line has served as my mantra: *"Life is a banquet and most poor sons of bitches are starving to death."* Yes, I was always hungry. I canceled nothing.

Just to add one more detail to the complicated story, as the French farce finished its run, I took on another acting commitment to play the role of Tanya in the musical, *Mamma Mia.* In defense of my sanity, I tried to refuse the role, but the director was extremely persuasive and I really wanted one more chance to work with my friends before I moved away. Plus, it was a really fun role to play. With my husband's blessing, I made it work. (His comment was, "You'll hate yourself if you don't do this." He knows me well.) I started rehearsing a few weeks before the move, but then the real challenge began. In between unpacking boxes and learning my way around my new home, I started commuting 300 miles to rehearsals and 300 miles home again. Luckily, the director supplied housing arrangements, so I could leave North Carolina on Thursday morning and return on Sunday afternoon. The other cast members were lenient and worked around me during the rehearsals that were held earlier in the week. I learned my choreography and music through the magic of technology. As crazy at the schedule seemed, I was still in my comfort zone. It was a great distraction from the drudgery of unpacking boxes. *I admit, I loved the crazy pace of my new life.* The irony behind this experience is the dilemma of the main character in *Mamma Mia.* After living twenty years as a single mother, Donna confronts the three men who are all possible baby-daddies. Oh, how the Universe was laughing.

The reason for this digression is to explain how I almost missed meeting my half-siblings. As I've said before, I don't have many acquaintances who were adopted as children. I haven't even watched the popular television shows that feature reunions. Although I'd spent a significant amount of time fantasizing about discovering siblings, I never thought it would really happen. Suddenly I experienced emotional anxiety. How, exactly, would I react? It was time for self reflection, a practice I was reticent to begin. My practical Yankee upbringing had discouraged examination of emotions, so I tended to avoid self-analysis whenever possible. My mind started to wander and wonder...Was I treating the situation as just another piece of theater in my life? As much as I hated to admit a personal failing, I had to acknowledge my common practice of emotional avoidance. It was true - my habit of immersing myself in personal chaos was a way to avoid processing true emotions. I wonder if this is a trait inherited from my birth mother. It seems like another logical conclusion. In a Freudian way, it could also explain how I mixed up the days of our meeting.

In the midst of relocating and rehearsing, I took time out for my trip to Massachusetts. At least I was traveling by plane this time. I have a lot of energy, but one more long drive might have finally done me in. I had received a few confirmation texts from Marc, and one stated that Barbie had suggested we meet at a "lobster in the rough" restaurant in Essex, Massachusetts. This was the first time I heard about Barbie's inclusion in the loop, and I was psyched. At the same time, I now had more questions.

I didn't know much about Barbie or where she fit into the new family picture. I wondered if Barbie felt like she had come late to the party. By the time her name had appeared on our Ancestry.com page, the saga of the long-lost siblings was old news. I sent her an email as soon as I saw her profile on my page, but like her half sister Cori, she didn't respond right away. Thankfully, a second email was more successful. She apologized for her negligence and admitted to feeling ambivalent about the whole situation. I wouldn't have suspected otherwise. At my expression of empathy she assured me, "It's okay. My relationship with my mother was tenuous at best." I later learned that Barbie had always wondered what caused her mother's prolonged absences. Now she had an answer, but one with more questions attached. Like mother, like daughter – Louise created chaos of her own, and the repercussions trickled down for more than half a century.

Now that I had finally made connections with several biological family members, I collected enough background stories to cobble together a history of the family Louise created. It was fractured and contained lots of holes, but it helped me understand Barbie's sense of ambivalence. Here's my understanding of the big picture: During the mid to late 1950's, Barbie was raised by her grandparents in Maine while Louise was busy breeding. Depending on the number of children actually placed for adoption, that time period could have lasted at least six years. Contrary to Louise's testimonial at the adoption agency, Barbie described her grandfather as a loving and devoted man. Her grandparents provided Barbie with a fully enriched childhood. She took dance lessons, enjoyed friends and referred to that time period as quite wonderful. The only uncertainty in Barbie's life surrounded her mother. Of course Louise's absences were confusing to a child, especially one who heard her mother lament, "They're trying to take you away from me". As an adult, I realized that this comment could be motivated by a number of variable factors. Were Louise's parents actively seeking legal guardianship, or was Louise merely reacting to an imagined threat? Since only Louise would be able to clarify, I can only speculate. But Barbie's ambivalent feelings are understandable.

I assume that Louise's life during that time was an emotional roller coaster. The fluctuation of hormone levels alone would have wreaked havoc on the emotions of any mother, never mind one who had bore four children in eight years without a spouse. I was relieved to learn that Louise finally achieved stability with a fine man. They were happily married for over thirty years. I'm pleased that she found a soul mate, but his entrance into her life is not without an unusual twist.

According to Betsy's recollection, Louise eventually reconciled with her parents. As a matter of fact, when her father became ill with cancer, Louise assumed the role of primary caretaker. Somewhere within this time frame, Louise's father introduced her to the love of her life. It's almost as if he had hand-picked her husband, and it's nice to think that the relationship between Louise and her father had come full circle. Still, it's unusual to think of a father playing Cupid for a daughter.

Louise finally achieved family stability with her new husband, and she had the opportunity to rebuild her life. Like any family, the dynamics became firmly established. I was told that Cori assumed the role of the most responsible sibling. Exerting their family status as oldest and youngest, Barbie and Jessica were said to be the most mischievous. In their own words, they indicated that Cori was the one who reeled them in. It makes sense that Cori would now be the sibling who lives closest to her widowed mother and serves as her primary caretaker. This is in keeping with her

160

character. At school, she works with Special Education students, she is a devoted mom and grandmother, and she is also raising one of her husband's nieces. It's obvious that she shares my penchant for multitasking, juggling a myriad of details at any given time. Her hands are more than full, and it appears that her heart is, too. I refuse to add any more pressure to her busy life, so I won't pry for more information than what is offered. Still, I hoped to add more pieces to the puzzle on June 23rd.

As I mentioned before, I almost missed the opportunity to meet with my biological family. What happened was totally my fault: a combination of mathematical confusion and extreme flakiness. On Thursday night, which I thought was June 20th, I was finally relaxing in Cape Cod and chatting with my Sidebottom family relatives. They knew most of my story and were fascinated - looking forward to hearing about my Saturday afternoon meet and greet. As usual, I had orchestrated a plan - starting with my arrival at my friend Kathy's house on Saturday morning by 8:30 am. We'd get to Woodman's restaurant by 1:00 with time to spare. The weather forecasters predicted a beautiful day, and I was looking forward to catching up with my friend during the scenic drive. On Friday, Marc texted me a reminder. It said, "Can't wait to see you on Sunday." Suddenly, I stopped in my tracks. Sunday? For two months, I had been planning to meet on Saturday. I wondered when I had last consulted a calendar. I had been so proud of my multitasking skills - juggling so many plates for so many months. Apparently "pride goeth before a fall" carries some truth. Suddenly, I was humbled - my little pea brain had almost screwed up this whole event. It's a good thing that Marc sent that text. (*the universe was at work again*) Otherwise, I would have arrived on the wrong day and thought my family had stood me up. In our own crazy way, Kathy and I would have managed to have a great girl's weekend, but still... At this point, at least my sense of humor kicked in. I couldn't wait to tell Kathy that I had mixed up the date. She's familiar with my occasional bout of flakiness, and she knows that numbers are not my friends.

Kathy has known me long enough to anticipate my catastrophes, and she had a great laugh over my latest mix-up. They never cease to amuse her. She has watched me drive my car away with my purse on the roof more than once. We have a history of taking what we call "Serendipity Tours" during summer road trips. That's basically a big word for getting lost, but finding somewhere else that's much more interesting. It happens to us quite frequently. For example, we toured Mount Vernon in Virginia one day because we couldn't figure out how to get off the rotary in Washington, D.C. So the current confusion didn't surprise Kathy a bit, and we just switched our itinerary to Plan B. Saturday was going to be a great day to tour downtown Salem. We'd eat our lobster on Sunday.

Sunday, June 23rd was a beautiful day on the North Shore of Massachusetts. We decided to head out early and enjoy the scenery before meeting my new family for lunch. We toured a little bit in the quaint towns of Gloucester and Northampton, Massachusetts, before heading for Woodman's restaurant in Ipswich. By the way, the town of Ipswich is world famous for its succulent clams, and cooks at Woodman's Restaurant were the first to fry them. A big surprise to some people is the fact that true New Englanders eat their clams whole, with the bellies attached. To me, a clam strip is just a poor man's substitute for calamari. The bigger draw at Woodman's, however, is their lobster, served boiled in the shell with lots of butter. Eating a lobster is messy business, so the service and seating is casual, featuring long wooden tables. Some of Woodman's tables are located under a huge tent near the rear of the building. It was a self-service operation, so patrons lined up in front, placed their orders and carried them to their seats.

Marc's suggestion to gather at one of the tables under the tent was a perfect idea. We would be assured some privacy, and we wouldn't be bothering anyone if we stayed a while. Kathy and I arrived a few minutes early. As we approached the tent, I thought I saw a man who I thought could be Marc. I announced to Kathy, "Oh my God, I think he's my brother!" I was about to embarrass myself by accosting a perfect stranger until Kathy reminded me that I had never seen Marc in person. She gently suggested that maybe I should hold back a minute to be sure. Of course she was right. Turns out it wasn't him, and she saved us both from potential embarrassment. That's what friends are for.

Shortly thereafter, I received a text saying that Marc and Sharon were stuck in traffic. I texted back saying that Kathy and I were hanging out under the tent. Marc's text was immediately followed by one from Ronno that said, "We're in the gift shop, but we'll be right there." Ronno was here? I had no idea that they were in on this plan. Since my 62nd birthday had been less than a week ago, I thought this might be one giant birthday surprise. Looking back on the situation, however, I think I just hadn't checked the text threads carefully. It was one more detail, like the date, that I had overlooked.

I recognized the group as they walked across the lawn. (After all, I had stalked their Facebook pages.) The next thing I knew I was engulfed in a huge family hug. Cori was accompanied by her very sweet husband, Bill, and Ronno had brought along his girlfriend Shannon. I'm not sure what I expected to feel - maybe an electrical current traveling through my body as my brain registered the shock - but it all just felt comfortable.

The first noticeable difference between us all was in height. Cori and Ronno were at least five inches shorter than me. Although I am only 5' 7 inches tall, I felt like an Amazon among the family group. This was especially true when the next half-sister arrived. Barbie showed up sporting long braided hair and a very tall significant other. Although she was the oldest, she was by far the most diminutive at 4' 10". Her frame was fine-boned and she seemed almost fragile. I was shocked at how much she physically resembled my youngest daughter. I've always been surprised that my daughters never grew to be taller than 5' 3", and unlike anyone on my husband's side of the family, my youngest daughter Kristin has a tiny bone structure. Her Senior prom gown had been a size 0. This newly-discovered gene pool now explained that phenomenon. The baby of the family, Jessica, arrived next with her husband Frank. Although they had different birth-fathers, she resembled Cori. Finally, Marc and his wife arrived. He was more than six feet tall, but my arms were happy to stretch up for a hug. We were so fortunate to have my friend Kathy along because she is a talented photographer, and she captured every embrace. She also arranged us in a series of group pictures. We posed in birth order, in height order, and we even shot a picture that left space for "Jane Doe" and our other brother, David. When we realized that all of us were born with an elongated second toe, we took off our shoes so she could photograph our feet, too.

All totaled, there were thirteen of us from two generations. I think it's interesting to note that only Marc, Cori and I have children. Certainly sociologists could draw all kinds of conclusions about that detail. Marc brought his daughter, and Cori brought her son, so cousins had a chance to meet. We reserved two picnic benches under the tent and headed to the front of the restaurant to get our meals. Marc and I, of course, had longer legs than most, so we got to the order line before anyone else. Because Woodman's is so popular and the June afternoon was so lovely, the line was long. It was a while before our shorter-legged siblings caught up to us, but we cut them into the line. That's what families do, right? Yikes! I noticed a woman behind me counting heads as eleven people jumped in front of them. My fear of confrontation inspired some quick improvisation, and I immediately invited her and her friend to please step ahead of us. Kathy jumped to my assistance and explained the reason for the gathering. The woman and her friend were charmed to have witnessed a DNA event. Had we had our wits about us, we might have recorded it for future Ancestry.com advertisement, but we were too busy salivating over thoughts of fresh lobster.

The food was great, and the company was better. Marc and I enjoyed watching our half siblings exchange sarcastic barbs at one another - the easy teasing attitude of those who grew up together - but I think he would agree that we never felt left out. It was impossible to talk or hear all thirteen of us at once, so we rotated seats every now and then. I think it was Jessica who reminded us that this was just like speed dating. Anecdotes from childhood were generously shared. I took special note when I heard that Louise had been very strict about her children's behavior. They each remembered being warned against "bringing shame to the family name." Withholding judgement as much as possible, I can't help but notice the irony in this admonition, and I detected a few sarcastic snickers among the crowd. Exactly what was the motivation behind Louise's cautionary message? Was it merely a phrase that had been embedded in her head during her adolescence? Or was this a subliminal acknowledgment of her own past actions? ("Do as I say, not as I do?") Was she protecting her husband's good name? Or was she just trying to be a conscientious mother? Here are more questions to add to the myriad of unknowns in the life of Louise.

Marc and I clung to the elucidating tidbits of information supplied by our half siblings. Cori related a recent eerie experience where Louise mentioned Marc's birth name. One day she told her mother that she was expecting a grandson. When she asked her opinion about a name, Louise answered, "I've always liked the name Dale Edward." Cori knew that was the birth name Louise had given Marc. Wow! Cori wished she had thought fast enough to initiate further discussion, but by the time she recovered, her mother was discussing a different topic. That's the closest Louise ever came to mentioning even the tiniest detail about her adopted children.

As the afternoon wore on, it became clear that my birth father was the giant elephant in the room. I knew that everyone present had discovered the story one way or another, but there was an obvious level of uncertainty surrounding my emotional attachment to the facts. I think everyone was trying to protect my feelings, as devoted siblings would. Finally, somebody broke the ice. It was Jessica, the spunky, self-proclaimed spoiled baby of the family who brought it up. She made a humorous suggestion about playing a family game of "Who's Your Daddy?" I assured everyone at the table that I hadn't been traumatized by my father's identity, just fascinated. Much conjecture ensued which ended with a synchronous sigh of "What was Mama doing?"

Ronno then brought up the topic of the mysterious "Donald" described so thoroughly in my adoption records. All of a sudden, somebody remembered that Louise sometimes talked about her high school boyfriend whose name was Donald. Was this the same guy? Louise hadn't been out of high school more than five years when I was born. Had she reunited with him? Did she hope to? Was she hoping I would bring them together? Did she think Donald was my father? Or had William Bradford Bishop called himself Donald? Anything was possible.

The fact that none of her children had confronted Louise was a testament to her family's devotion. Each was protective in his or her own way. We heard that David, the half-brother who lived in Colorado, was no longer in the dark. Jessica admitted that she had recently filled him in. According to her, he responded with, "Well, that explains a lot." Nobody offered any clarification of that remark, and I didn't think it was appropriate to ask. I still wonder what he meant.

I was as careful as I could be to keep positive communication lines open with my new-found family. Although my siblings shared a healthy dose of sarcasm, and some biting comments were made regarding Louise's secret life, I managed to curb my own naturally sarcastic nature. It was never my place to judge or criticize. As a daughter and a mother, I respect the many nuances of that relationship. The very presence of Marc and myself already spoke volumes about their mother's past.

No mysteries would be solved at this meeting, but we were now real to each other. This past year brought a paradigm shift upon the entire family, and all have responded with grace. Perhaps that is my birth-mother's legacy: grace. Having met these half-siblings in the flesh, I share their feeling of loyalty and commend their compassion toward Louise. I like to think we share that in our DNA.

I don't think Marc or I will ever meet our birth mother, and I think both of us are okay with that. Marc suggested that we each write a letter to her.

Actually, his first suggestion was a birthday card on March 13th signed by Dale Edward and Darlene Marie. That idea was dismissed as too dramatic, but it morphed into a simple thank you note. We hoped Cori would keep them under wraps until an appropriate time presented itself. It seemed like a good plan that would provide closure and satisfy our original goal.

I also don't think that Louise's version of the story will ever be told. I've accepted that fact. Jessica, her youngest child, said that she was "just going to have to go ask mom about all this," None of her siblings voiced encouragement, so I don't think they supported the idea. And even if Jessica did confront Louise, I doubt that she would get any concrete answers; at least not in the near future. Our mother is still in mourning, and she is adjusting to a new lifestyle. Although she is in good health, I'm sure her emotional well-being is fragile. We have no way of telling whether or not she will ever grow stronger. Ronno's prediction might just be right. We all might just have to respect his grandmother and allow her to take her secrets with her to the grave.

Part Five
Life Goes On

A year has passed since I met my biological family, and I cannot say that our lives have significantly changed. As much as I abhor the overused phrase, "It is what it is," I think it's an appropriate conclusion. There has been lots of drama. We have all survived a journey of discovery, accepted scientific evidence and expanded our sense of identity. We've been provided with an opportunity to broaden our perspectives and reevaluate relationships. I'm sure we all agree that our lives are fuller, but not different. We are still the same people and we are living the same lives, but those lives have been enriched through biology.

A benefit of my journey is that I've learned to trust my instincts, and I'm mindful of what I used to refer to as coincidence. Some people say there are no coincidences in life, and maybe that's true - I'm not sure. There are a few things, however, that I am sure about: Who I am is the sum of many parts, some acquired through nurture and some by nature. I now view my identity in simple dramatic terms. *Surprise!* I've always been the star of my show. What I learned about my birth parents proves that I was born with a predetermined genetic disposition: characteristics I inherited from Brad and Louise. We are genetically connected. Norma and Jack provided the context. We are consciously connected. They are all members of my supporting cast. My actions and decisions formed the plot of the drama, and it's the intermingling of these elements that created the story of my life. It's not a case of nature vs nurture; it's nature + nurture that solidified my identity.

I'm glad I followed through with my search. My only regret is that I didn't have a chance to thank my birth mother. I never wrote her a letter, but I recently learned that Marc did. He composed a note and sent it on to Cori. In it, he thanked her for her actions and assured her that he lived a happy, productive life. I wish I had done the same thing, but now it's too late. Unfortunately, Louise passed away in the Spring. I like to think that she now has the opportunity to check in on all of us, and I hope she feels proud.

I would be remiss if I didn't take one more opportunity to stress the serious nature of a DNA search. I haven't inspected a test kit lately, but I think each one should contain a cautionary note for the user: Be careful what you look for. The information I discovered was fascinating and powerful. It created an entertaining story, but it also disrupted the emotions and reputations of people I had never met before.. Although my intentions were innocent, I experienced a large amount of guilt for creating chaos. I was lucky to have been forgiven - by myself and by my half sisters and brothers. Others might not be so fortunate.

Many of the mysteries underscored in this story are still unsolved. Of course I would love to know if Brad Bishop is dead or alive. I'd like to see a DNA comparison of crime scene evidence with my own, just to have that concrete piece of proof. I can't help but wonder how Brad and Louise got together, and I'd love to know the details of their relationship. I still hope that the unknown sibling mentioned in my adoption document will surface, and I'd love to know who her father is. Perhaps this book will prompt some answers. But maybe not.

Right now I'm satisfied with what I know, and I'm at peace with what I don't know. My original goal was to find out who I am, and I feel much closer to reaching that goal. Any future discoveries will be embraced as icing on the cake. I'm always happy to add new characters to my story as long as the plot continues to follow this path toward a happy ending. I'm reminded once again of the words of the Bishops' family friend, Jacques D'Amboise, "Let us spend as much time as possible with the Good and doing Good." It's all good.

*Addendum

And Now For the Rest of the Story... by Susan Tupper Gillmor.

The Genetic Genealogy Approach

Let me begin with a brief summary of Genetic DNA testing from Wikipedia to outline in a general way the process involved in using DNA to discover family connections between and among different family groups (https://en.wikipedia.org/wiki/Genealogical_DNA_test):

"A **genealogical DNA test** is a DNA-based test which looks at specific locations of a person's genome, in order to find or verify ancestral genealogical relationships or (with lower reliability) to estimate the ethnic mixture of an individual. Since different testing companies use different ethnic reference groups and different matching algorithms, ethnicity estimates for an individual will vary between tests, sometimes dramatically.

Three principal types of genealogical DNA tests are available, with each looking at a different part of the genome and useful for different types of genealogical research: autosomal, mitochondrial (mtDNA), and Y-DNA.

Autosomal tests may result in a large amount of DNA matches (other test persons that the individual may be related to), along mixed male and female lines, each match with an estimated distance in the family tree. However, due to the random nature of which and how much DNA is inherited by each tested person from their common ancestors, precise conclusions can only be made for close relations. Traditional genealogical research, and the sharing of family trees, is typically required for interpretation of the results. Autosomal tests are also used in estimating ethnic mix."

It is autosomal DNA that is in play with most of the popular DNA testing sites today, like 23andme.com and Ancestry.com. And it's autosomal DNA and these specific sites that connected Kathy and me in the first place. Both 23andme and Ancestry process saliva samples and in a few weeks give us back a list of all the people on their testing database who share measurable samples of DNA segments that prove a familial relationship between us. The lists proffered range from the closest relations (those with the largest numbers of centimorgans - abbreviated as cMs, the unit of measure for these shared DNA chromosome segments) to the most distant.

There are handy dandy charts for estimating the average number of cMs for various generational relationships. Beyond parent/child matches (which are always around 3500 shared cMs), the more distant the relationship, the broader the range of shared cMs. First cousins average 874 cMs, second cousins average 233 cMs, third cousins average 74 cMs on the chart I usually use. Kathy came in at a 145 cMs shared match on our initial 23andme match list. As she says, we were in touch very quickly and I never let go of the search until we knew everything that was worth knowing. To this day I keep my eyes peeled for that one loose end remaining (Jane Doe), or anything else unexpected to turn up. The unexpected has been the theme of this particular genetic genealogy process.

It just so happens I'd already encountered a few adoptees for whom I'd been able to help determine biological parents. AND I already had an extensive paper tree on Ancestry that included the siblings and offspring for as many of my great-grandparents, great-great-grandparents, great-great-great grandparents and so on going back through the generations as far as is feasible or possible. One common mistake many new DNA testers make is they think their match lists will magically build them a neat family tree. Not so. A well-developed paper tree using traditional genealogical methods must be used in tandem.

I can guarantee that most people have very few, if any, DNA matches who share their surname (or direct paternal line). In my several years of DNA genealogy, I have found two people with the Tupper surname, and one of them was adopted and matched me on a different family branch. Every single person, without exception, who is more distantly related than sibling will be related to us through the descendants of the siblings of our direct ancestors. First cousins are descendants of our parents' siblings. Second cousins are related through descendants of the siblings of our grandparents, and so on and so forth. Once one of those siblings is a female, her descendants will bear her married surname and I probably won't recognize it.

To illustrate my point another way, my Tuppers are just one family line among many on my paternal side alone. By the time I get to my great-great-grandparents, I'm juggling eight different paternal branches/surnames. That number doubles every single generation. Well, unless your ancestors comprised limited numbers of family groups in isolated rural areas and they often interbred out of sheer necessity, in which case things can get complicated quickly. (More on this later.) But then figure in all the siblings and their spouses and children and there are now dozens more surnames than eight (at the great-great grand level) that must be considered.

So Kathy appears on my match list on 23andme on June 1, 2017, estimated to be in a 2nd to 3rd cousin range of shared DNA. A note from her alerts me to this new match that morning. Any close match is exciting, but adoptees are my favorite matches. I was gifted with a deep sense of my own roots, deep in Maine soil and early northern New England settlement history. I can't even imagine not knowing where I come from. I believe in my heart that everybody has the right to know who their people are, what genes they possess in every cell in their bodies, what their unique family history contains, in short, where they come from. With DNA technology there are no more secrets and I'm committed to help anyone who crosses my path discover their own history and roots, if they choose to know. At the same time, I believe that everyone (birth parents included) has the right to not establish contact with a parent or child if that is too painful or complicated for them.

So first off, in my efforts to provide Kathy with her very own biological family roots, I used an essential tool that tells me which people we share in common on our separate match lists. Our shared match list included cousins whom I'd already identified (phew!) and I knew right off that we were looking at surnames like Berry, Andrews, Cates, Flynn, Schoppe, all of which are part of my broader paternal grandfather's Tupper family branch. They could appear in present day generations as many other names, depending on marriages, name changes, etc. And wouldn't you know, that particular set of families is from an isolated rural area with high levels of interbreeding in its settlement past (and up to the present day), so a possibility existed that Kathy and I could be related through more than one main branch of my family. (My paternal Tupper grandfather is also related to my paternal grandmother.) My work was now cut out for me.

First I had to go to my Ancestry tree to figure out which separate branches might have produced a mother or a father for Kathy. We had no idea at this point which gender my family had provided to her parental gene pool. Because Kathy was either a 2nd cousin or 3rd cousin (or somewhere in-between, say a 2nd cousin once removed), I started checking different individual lines within the targeted section of my tree that may have produced a son or daughter the right age to be Kathy's biological parent. I'm easily looking at dozens - if not hundreds - of separate twigs on those branches that could conceal the key to Kathy's genetic identity.

I had a copy of the non-identifying document (NII) Kathy was given by the adoption agency and kept my eye on that as I searched. According to this info given to the adoption agency way back when, the bio father was named Donald and the bio mother was Louise. I found a couple of Donalds, but neither had sons who could be Kathy's half-brothers and they were probably too old and had been married at the time Kathy was conceived. There was one Donald who was my dad's second cousin who had also been his friend. But I thought he was very unlikely because none of the other factors jived with a Baby Daddy for Kathy. And then I found a branch with a man who could fulfill several of the characteristics of the adoption document. He would have been the right age and he did have two sons that could be Kathy's half-brothers. But his name wasn't Donald, it was Clayton. A woman of that time who was pregnant out of wedlock had to have been under a lot of stress. It wouldn't be unusual to give incorrect information on adoption agency forms. So I went with Clayton and shared the info with Kathy.

We had now eliminated one solid possibility, and I had met a few 2nd cousins whom I'd never known before and that's always a treat! But I was back at square one in the grand quest for Kathy's birth parents. I was pretty sure at this point that our search was geographically confined to Washington County, Maine. Kathy was born and given up for adoption in the Boston area, but I believed that at least one of her birth parents was likely born in Downeast Maine. Since my tree is quite extensive and my paternal line traces back to early Colonial history in the 17th century, I was convinced that one of her grandparents had to be on my tree already, but that grandparent may have married someone who probably wasn't on my tree or biologically related to me. So I extended my search to find that other grandparent. He or she WOULD certainly be represented on Kathy's match list - somewhere.

By now Kathy had taken the Ancestry DNA test and the database there is much larger than that of 23andme. Kathy gave me full access to her list and I began building what are called mirror trees, separate little trees for common names I'm finding in the trees of other DNA matches. Some of the common names I was finding all revolved around the location of Lubec, Maine, a town which happens to boast the distinction as the Easternmost town in the USA. It's a bit east of the Machias area where most of my family settled, but close enough to easily find a marriage partner there. Surnames included Gray and Griffin and Ouellette and I built trees for each of them. Sure enough, Grays guided me to a marriage with a Griffin and then with an Ouellette. I was sure these families were all connected to "other" grandparent I was seeking. The excitement mounted.

Keep in mind that this process has now taken several months and includes a couple of detours and dead-ends. But finally it felt like I was on the right track. Ancestry.com is marvelous. So many vital records and other family material has been digitalized that much genealogical research can happen without leaving our computer chairs. And I was also now in contact with other cousins from Kathy's match list who were related through families other than mine, all from the Downeast Maine locations I expected. Somewhere their families had to connect with mine.

One day in early 2018 another of Kathy's cousins on the Gray/Griffin/Ouillette side provided me with an obituary for a Gray family member. In a long list of loved ones of the deceased which also included those Ouillettes and Griffins, my eye zeroed in on the name "Tupper." It appeared as a middle name for a close family relative. Bingo! It's highly unlikely that anyone would give their kid the middle name of Tupper if they're not an official member of our tribe. My excitement level soared, my energy was reborn, and I took this new specific name right to my tree. And there he was, the son of my Tupper great-grandfather's sister. [I've found that graph paper works well for generational charting, in case you're having trouble tracking this information.]

So this man with the Tupper middle name was a first cousin of my own dear grandfather. I found a marriage record for him and that couple had one child, a daughter named Louise who was born and grew up on the North shore of Massachusetts. When we're on the right path in a DNA search, all parts of the puzzle start to fall effortlessly into place, and that's what was happening now. That location was perfect. Kathy was born in Boston. Louise would be my father's 2nd cousin. I could now call Kathy and announce - "It's a girl! And you're officially my third cousin!"

Finding a Father

It took a few months to find Kathy's birth mother, but the process was relatively simple because I was working with my own large, well-developed family tree. Louise was related to me, too. After that task was accomplished (ongoing surprises surfacing on Louise's side notwithstanding), Kathy still didn't have the identity of her birth father. I'd naively believed we'd get that information from the mother once she was identified. Louise was still living, and that should be easy, right? Wrong. Nothing about finding Kathy's roots has been all that easy. And the unsolved mystery around Kathy's paternity never strayed far away from my consciousness.

So one day in late Spring of 2018 I found myself packing up my entire apartment for a temporary move to a nearby studio while they overhauled my unit. I was hot, frustrated, tired and badly in need of an enjoyable diversion. I booted up my laptop, dove deeply into Kathy's match list, and was determined to stick with it until I'd succeeded in my Grand Quest to find her a father.

For those paying attention to the methodology above, you'll understand that I was now searching for duplicate family names and other discernible patterns in the trees of Kathy's DNA matches, particularly geographic locations. I made lists of the Ancestry matches who were also related to each other. By now I was able to separate most of her maternal matches from her paternal matches in her closer relatives (up to 3rd cousins or even 4th cousins who shared higher than average cMs of DNA). I wrote notes to several of the 2nd and 3rd cousins who might be willing to aid me in the search.

I now added Kathy's raw DNA data to a site called GEDmatch.com, an indispensable clearinghouse for DNA results from all the major testing companies. GEDmatch not only offers a larger match list of DNA cousins, but also offers valuable tools for locating family groups among those matches. I needed all the tools I could find. The website has made news in the past couple of years because of its use as a tool for law enforcement to successfully find and prosecute unsolved violent crimes. The Golden State Killer is perhaps the best known of these dangerous fugitives brought to justice through the use of genetic genealogy. I was using the exact same website and methods, but with the more modest goal of simply finding a birth father, not a dangerous criminal....

Kathy's father will have two parents, 4 grandparents, 8 great-grandparents, and so forth. I'm hoping to find duplicate names among Kathy's DNA matches that will allow me to separate different family groups that correspond to these various grands and great-grands. The process of finding them is not linear and involves a lot of dead ends and going back and forth between little mirror trees. In the case of this particular search, I found one common ancestral name in three different trees of fairly close cousins - St. Germain. Although the given names were different, two of the trees traced back to a common ancestral couple in a specific area of Quebec with migrations to Minnesota.

It may sound extremely helpful to find this surname in common, but French-Canadian families tend to be much bigger than those of other families of Northern European ancestry and can prove far more difficult to find connecting links between various branches. But since this was all I had to work with, I began to build small mirror trees using this surname from the accessible trees of Kathy's matches. The genealogy gods were smiling on me this time and without an undue amount of time or effort, I found a common ancestral couple that tied these three trees together. And then I found siblings of this couple who were found in the trees of other DNA matches farther back. Those moments of discovery are magical! When pieces fall into place in this way, it's a great indication that we're on the right track. There was a great deal more work to do, but it was a good start and the French-Canadian origins of the St. Germains helped me make educated guesses that allowed me to tie other matches with French-Canadian names into the broader St. Germain tree.

In many ways, the type of genetic genealogy used to locate a biological parent from the DNA match list of an adoptee is a logic puzzle, if you will, perhaps akin to a game of Clue. I now have a name that I know must be somewhere on Kathy's family tree in the not-too-distant past. There are enough 2nd and 3rd and 4th cousins of Kathy's with the name St. Germain in their trees, that it's possible a great-grandparent, a grandparent, or even her parent MIGHT have the surname St. Germain. So is Kathy's paternal grandparent Mrs. St. Germain in Illinois from Springfield, or maybe Mr. St. Germain in

Minnesota from St. Paul? Not enough clues yet to make that determination.

I continued the search for other family groups. While the St. Germains seemed to be grouped in the northern tier of the Midwest, I was finding other surnames situated in Ohio and Illinois, some in the more Southern tier of Midwestern America and still others from the mid-Atlantic and the Deep South. Nothing was cohering very well until I spotted the name Corder on a few trees and the matches with Corder also shared DNA matches with others who had Hamblin/Hamblen in their trees. I created another mirror tree with those names and found an ancestor couple where a Corder man married a Hamlin woman (both born in the 1830s) and they migrated to Illinois and stayed there until they died. Because I know Kathy's age, this couple could easily be in the same generation as Kathy's great-great-grandparents - perhaps. I developed this tree in the same way I did the St. Germain tree. Finding siblings of all the generations I could locate and extending them as far toward the present day as is possible.

Another little group that seemed to connect to each other were a family of Smiths (usually greeted with groans for the obvious reasons) and one named Bishop. I found one woman named Smith (from two different matches' trees) whose family seemed unusually well-documented. Her father was born in Kentucky and died in Illinois. Both locations are resonating by now. This Smith woman married a man named Bishop (born in Ohio, died in Illinois also). So as I extend these families and this particular couple, suddenly I see that a Bishop son married a Corder daughter from my other mirror tree. The excitement mounts.

The Bishop/Corder marriage I found seems to produce only two sons, the older born in 1896 and the younger in 1899. If this is the line I'm looking for, either would be just about right to qualify as a grandfather of Kathy's. I'm almost holding my breath at this point. [A brief reminder that I am searching for a man named Donald to fulfill the information from Kathy's orphanage document.] The older Bishop son fathers only two daughters. I let out a groan of disappointment. But the younger son . . .

Is named William Bradford Bishop and marries a woman named Louisa May Corder. We are on a roll and the ball is rolling faster now. William Bradford Bishop marries Lobelia Amaryllis St. Germain. And they produce only one child, a boy named William Bradford Bishop Jr. I pour over all the branches on all the mirror trees I've constructed in my search, and he becomes the only possible candidate I can find who is very much the right age to be a father to Kathy.

I have a few doubts when I see he was born in Los Angeles County, California. Kathy's birth mother was in Massachusetts at the time of Kathy's birth. They couldn't live much farther apart than that. But then I noticed that during that time frame, Bishop Jr. was a student at Yale University in Connecticut. From New Haven to Boston would be a drive of 2 hours or so. Much more plausible now. I officially had a likely final clue to the puzzle - Mr. William Bradford Bishop Jr., in Boston, maybe at a frat party or night club!

Once I have a name for someone who could still be alive, I like to start with some good old-fashioned Facebook stalking. I typed the name into the Search box, rather doubting any results since this man would be in his 80s by now. Imagine the state of my face when up pops an FBI Most Wanted poster - with a photo of a man who looks so much like Kathy it's almost ridiculous. I regret that I didn't have the camera activated on my laptop. I'm fairly sure my jaw dropped to the keyboard and I know I uttered some version of WTF. And I think I shook my head several times in an effort to shake away this illusion in case I was just seeing things. But it was still there on the screen in living color. How in the blazes was I going to tell Kathy about discovering that her birth father killed his whole family in 1976 and has been an FBI fugitive ever since?

Kathy has a good head on her shoulders, a great sense of humor, and knowing these things helped me dial her number. Our memories differ somewhat about this momentous day and then we realized I remembered this first call better and Kathy remembers the second call in more detail. So here's how I remember that first call (paraphrasing is involved):

Me: Are you sitting down?

Kathy: Yes, I'm driving to Atlanta to meet up for lunch with some old friends.

Me: Aaaah. Ummmm. Maybe we need to talk later when you're not driving.

Kathy: Oh, no, no, no. I know you must have news. Spill!

Me: Well, the good news is I've found your father.

Kathy: Great! So who is he? Oh, wait, so what's the bad news?

Me: Well, he's on the FBI most wanted list as a fugitive from justice. He killed his whole family in 1976 and was never caught.

Kathy: (Long dead silence)

Me: (Holding my breath)

Kathy: I'M GOING TO HAVE THE BEST STORY AT LUNCH!!!

Me: (Laughing - relieved) Well, okay then!

And the rest is the history you've just finished reading.

Photographs/Documents

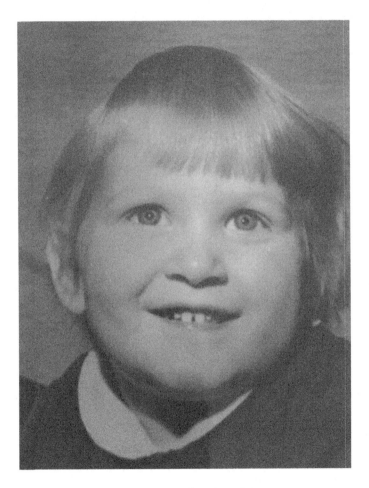

The author's first headshot

The crowning of Miss Stoughton, 1976

Heavy is the crown that wears the head?

The Miss Stoughton float at the 4th of July parade

Proud parents with the queen of the Stoughton
Sesquicentenial Ball

William Bradford Bishop

The photograph that appeared on his wanted poster

An artist's rendering of what Bishop might look like
today

Susan and I: Cousins meeting for the first time.

Norma and Jack Sidebottom on the 50th wedding
anniversary

Sept 25 2010

Dear Kathy ....

There is much in this memoir that touches on The
Bishops ---

Brad ... Lobelia ... annette ...

..... unexplainable? ... MADNESS! BRAIN TUMOR!
PARANOIA ..
MYSTERY! SATAN.
LUCIFER!
ABOVE ALL TRAGEDY.

LET US SPEND AS MUCH TIME AS POSSIBLE WITH THE Good and doing Good...

...inspiring children through the arts

may you have much JOY in your life ... Bye For Now Jacques d'amboise

Letter from J'acques D'Amboise

196

About the Author

Kathy Gillcrist has worked as an English and theater educator, actress and director for over 40 years. She studied acting at the Boston University School for the Arts, earned a M.A.T- English from Bridgewater State University, and an Ed. S degree from Piedmont College in Demorest, Georgia. She is the mother of two daughters and has been married to her husband, Paul, for 42 years. Originally from Massachusetts, she now resides in Carolina Shores, North Carolina where she continues to live a dramatic life.

Contributing Editor:

Susan Tupper Gillmor is a native of South Portland, Maine, who shares with Kathy early settler roots in coastal Massachusetts and Downeast Maine. She holds a B.A. in English Lit from University of Southern Maine in Portland, ME, and an M.A. in English from the University of Florida in Gainesville, FL. She inherits her love of genealogy and family history from her Tupper grandfather and has discovered the fun of DNA testing for finding family members. Helping adoptees find their biological families has become a particular passion of hers and this book comprises the best adoption story yet of her new avocation!

159

Made in the USA
Las Vegas, NV
11 March 2022

45470053R00115